THE COLLECTIVE EYE IN CONVERSATION WITH RUANGRUPA

Thoughts on Collective Practice

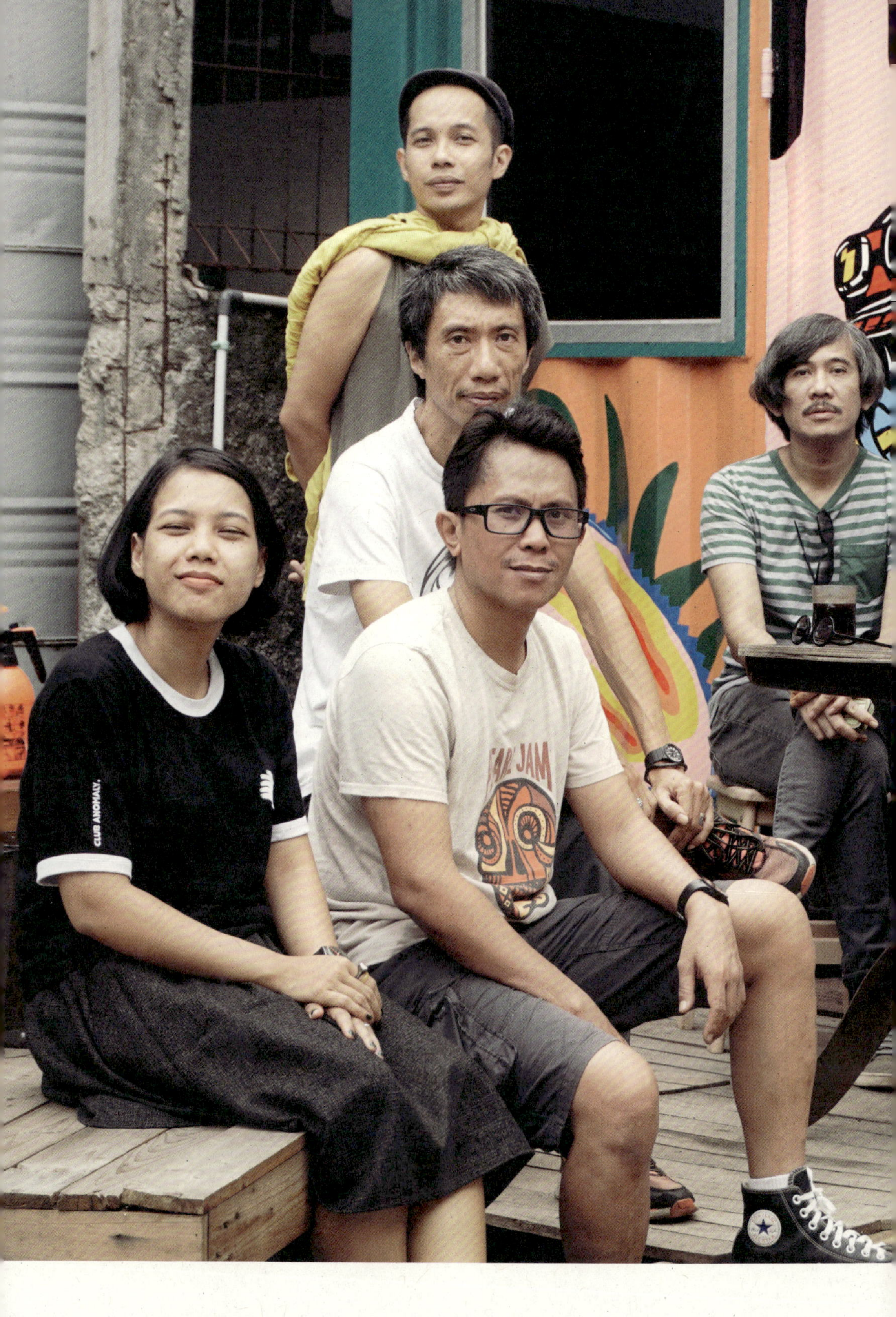
CLUB ANOMALY.
JAM

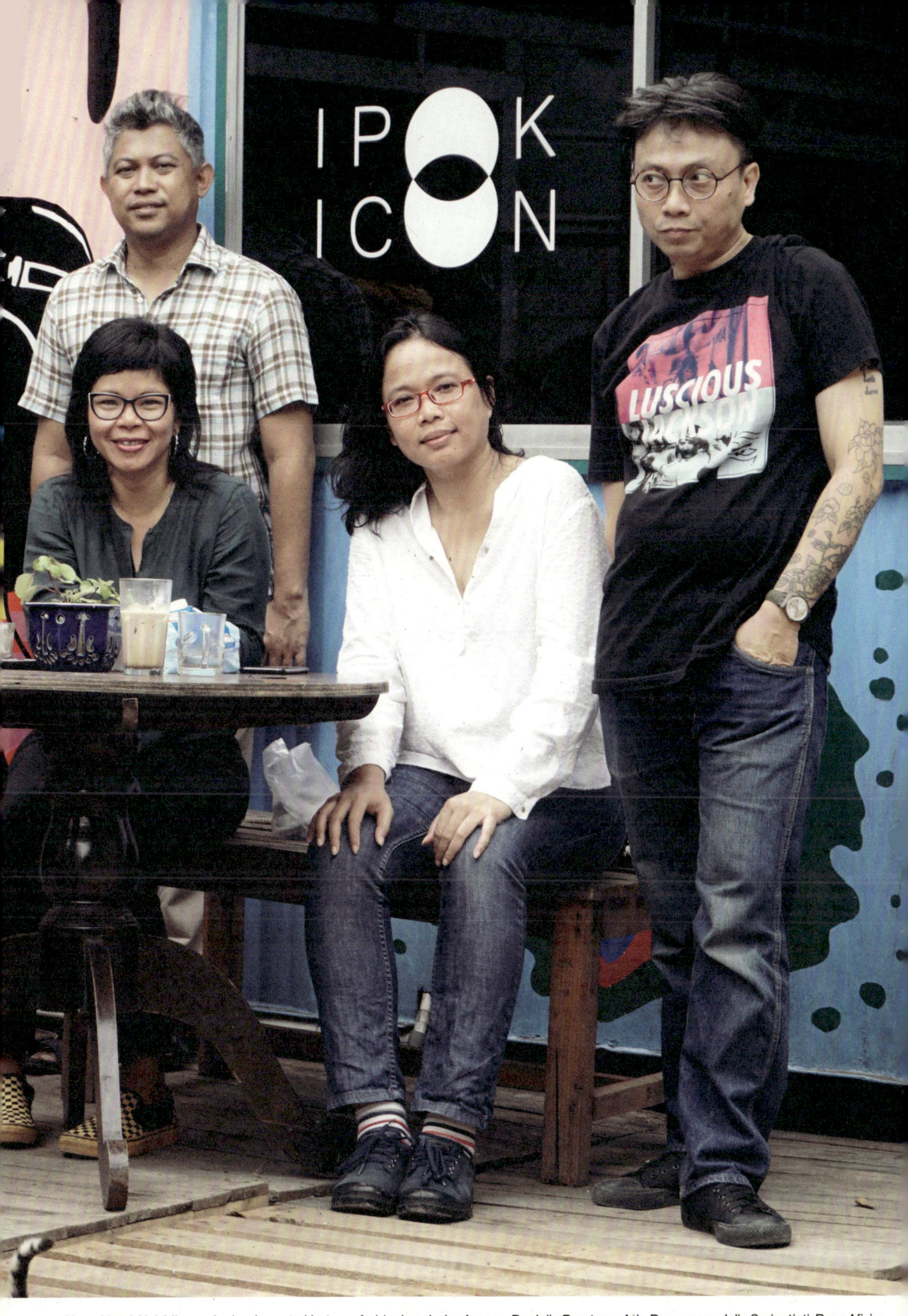

Ajeng Nurul Aini, Mirwan Andan, Iswanto Hartono, farid rakun, Indra Ameng, Daniella Praptono, Ade Darmawan, Julia Sarisetiati, Reza Afisina

CONTENTS

KNOWLEDGE, VALUES, AND RESPECT

This year's documenta–one of the world's largest and most influential art exhibitions–will be curated by a collective for the first time in its history. Another first: the artistic directors come from Asia. ruangrupa is an association of nine friends who unconditionally combine art with their everyday lives as a practice of living and surviving together under the socioeconomic conditions of their native Indonesia. Fourteen other collectives, so-called *lumbung members*, have been invited to join ruangrupa in transforming Kassel into a new, sustainable *ekosistem*. *lumbung*, the Indonesian term for a communal rice barn, is the starting point for all their activities and also this documenta.

The transformation and rewriting of history and authorship lie at the core of ruangrupa's artistic and curatorial projects. Their collective working method and practice is based on an alternative, community-oriented model of social, ecological, and economic sustainability. Everything is based on social participation. ruangrupa is a collective without a program founded in 2000. Instead, everything develops out of values like humor, generosity, and local anchoring–not out of idealized premises or superstructures, but rather the practice of living together.

What makes ruangrupa special is that they not only share ideas and knowledge, but also distribute their financial resources among all members and friends in the form of a basic income.

We talked to ruangrupa about their beginnings, the harsh struggle for survival under the Suharto regime in Indonesia, underground concerts, and student protests. About the euphoria after the dictatorship fell and the longing to come together and converse. About Jakarta as the perpetual wellspring of their shared drive. About punk, karaoke, and video culture. About early festivals, their first art projects, and the genesis of spaces like *gudskul*. About maintaining solidary social relationships, the Indonesian tradition of sharing, the collectivization of the world, and their unusual approach to resources–fascinated by the unlimited solidarity and friendship that not only holds the collective together. It is also the motor of everything they do and the goal behind networking with other collectives across the globe.

The autobiographical conversations are supplemented by five exemplary glimpses into some of ruangrupa's projects since 2003 and enriched with previously unpublished archival material as well as photographic impressions of their homeland.

We look forward to seeing how ruangrupa's practice will unfold and transform when seen through the lens of the international art world's attention in the context of this documenta. It is our hope that this volume of conversations can contribute to a deeper understanding of ruangrupa's subversive style of thinking and acting.

The Collective Eye and Matthias Kliefoth

1994 / 1995 → college time →

1996 / 1997 → meet Ade from

1997 / 1998 → monetary crisis, reform
1998 → Iswanto went to Jakart
1999 / 2000 → initiation of ruangrupa
→ ade's back from Rijksaka d
2000 → our first rented house
2002 - 2004 → our second rented house
2004 - 2006 → our third rented house
2007 - 2015 → our fourth rented house

2010 → decompression on ruangrupa
2011 → siasat guide on artist ini
2015 - 2016 → Gudang Sarinah E
Inaa's been working

2017 - present → GudSkul ecosy

karta Institute of the Arts

ndra, Daniella, Reza)

onesia Art Institute — Jogja

n era, student college movement

Institute of the arts but left for scholarship

nstitute of

ith Ade + 6 others friends as fonder

e

Tebet area South Jakarta

10th years aniversary

practices as

are

osystem with others 2 collectives

closely since 2004

tem.

Notes by Reza Afisina from the conversation with The Collective Eye in March 2022

GLOSSARY

The creation of social relationships and the questioning of (power) relations are central components of ruangrupa's practice. This includes the use of language and to understand it as a tool for developing new perspectives and ideas.

LUMBUNG

In Indonesian agriculture the term lumbung, in English "rice barn," refers to the place where a community stores the surplus from its harvest. In emergency situations, this surplus can be distributed among the entire community according to collectively defined criteria. ruangrupa uses the term metaphorically as a collective guideline for living and working together based on empathy, community, and an economically sustainable system in which resources are pooled and shared. lumbung is also the curatorial concept for documenta fifteen.

GUDSKUL

In 2018, the collectives ruangrupa, Serrum, and Grafis Huru Hara jointly founded Gudskul (Contemporary Art Collective and Ecosystem Studies) as a public platform. Conceived as a learning space, it is intended as a space for thinking and knowledge production that operates beyond formal educational criteria. Gudskul also enables economic self-organization by offering artistic services. Anyone active in Gudskul can thus receive a monthly salary.

EKOSISTEM

Whether within ruangrupa or intercollectively, as in the case of Gudskul practice, collaboration is based on a diversity of people, knowledge, skills, etc., whose mutual interconnectedness and networking of knowledge and resources form an ekosistem (Indonesian for ecosystem).

RURUHAUS

The ruruHaus is a place, a "living room", in Kassel that especially invites the inhabitants of Kassel as well as artists and collectives to collaborate and experiment during documenta fifteen. The collaboration and exchange are not bound to any form.

KNOWLEDGE MARKET

ruangrupa uses the term Knowledge Market to describe a practice in which people or groups enter into direct exchanges with each other according to certain guidelines with the goal of sharing their knowledge.

NEW ORDER

Indonesia's second president, Suharto, referred to his administration (1966–1998) as the New Order (Orde Baru) to distinguish it from his predecessor's reign. Suharto came to power in a coup supported by the United States. The general's authoritarian regime and his so-called New Order were marked, among other things, by massacres of the population (1965–1969). The economic crisis and student protests against the dictator led to Suharto's resignation in 1998.

ASIAN FINANCIAL CRISIS

In 1997 and 1998, many Asian countries – especially Indonesia, Thailand, South Korea, Malaysia, and the Philippines – were affected by a financial, monetary, and economic crisis.

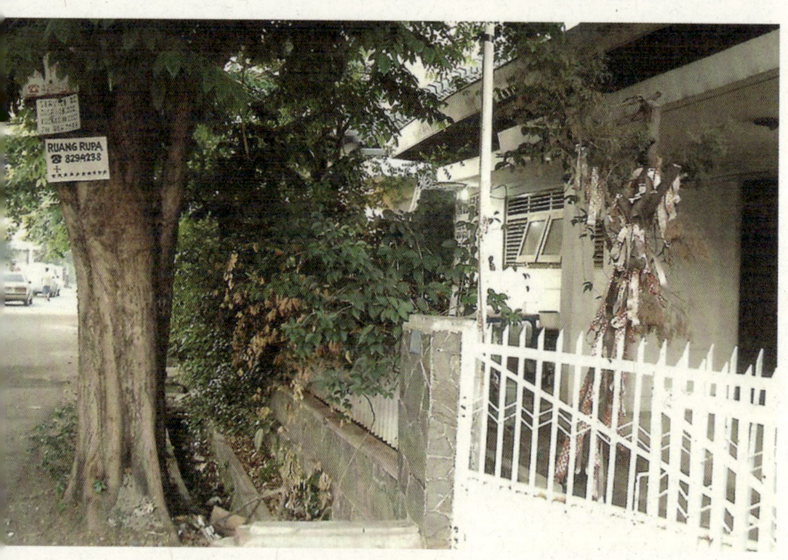

ruangrupa's first studio in a residential area in Jakarta, 2003

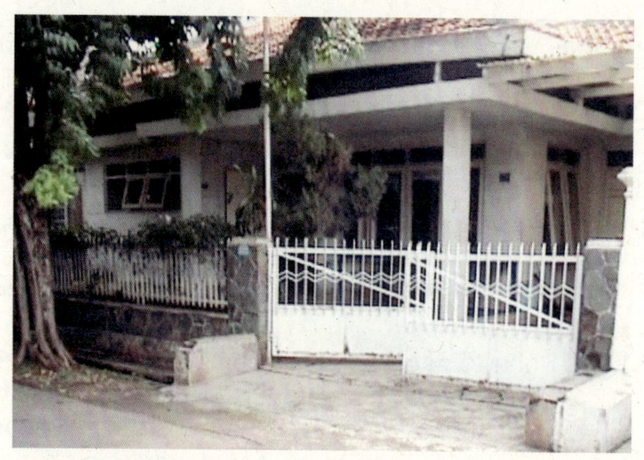

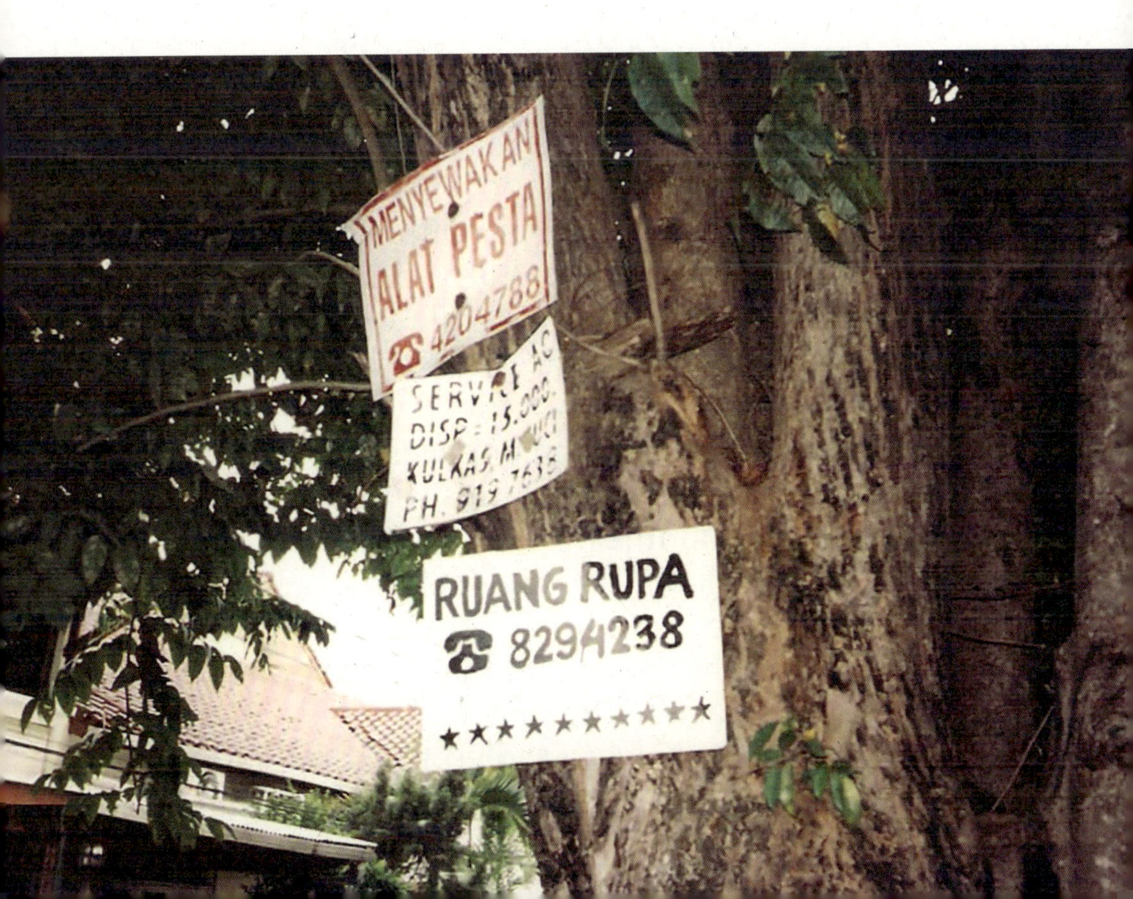
MENYEWAKAN
ALAT PESTA
4204788
SERVICE AC
DISP : 15.000.
KULKAS. M.CUCI
PH. 919 7636
RUANG RUPA
8294238

BORN FROM THE SPIRIT OF EVERYDAY LIFE: RUANGRUPA'S ORIGINS

IN CONVERSATION WITH ADE DARMAWAN

TCE Let's talk about your time back in art school and the origins of ruangrupa. How did it come about?

AD I was born and raised in Jakarta, but after high-school I studied at the art school in Yogyakarta, a place I'd describe as an educational and cultural city. It's smaller than Jakarta, but its art and culture scene is more vibrant. The city is in the center of Java. While I was there, many of my friends were studying in Jakarta. Reza, Indra, Daniella, and I–we've known each other for 27 years. I think it isn't just the longest relationship in our personal lives, but also more intense than our relationships with our families. We know each other's families.

After the era of the New Order regime ended, I started going back and forth between Yogyakarta and Jakarta. The student movement that led to Suharto being overthrown goes back to the time before independence. It has a long tradition. Our so-called founding fathers, the nationalist movement, were very young like us and came out of the student movement. At the end of the 1990s, we were activists at the art school, but only a very small part of a larger wave of protests. The protests also criticized the older generation, whom we denounced as corrupt, established, institutionalized, bureaucratic, feudal, and so on.

We felt really connected to this spirit and energy at the art schools, the Indonesian Institute of the Arts in Yogyakarta and the Jakarta Art Institute in Jakarta. We made publications like the magazine Karbon Journal, for example, as well as projects on the streets, and organized music concerts, but only very sporadically. Being a student back then was something completely different from what it is today. This also explains why we initiate a lot of projects in this area and maintain close contact with students, schools, and student life. Because that's how we grew up. We've always had this passion. For us, education isn't something trendy; talks and discussions were the order of the day, so we did a project called *Two Cities Dialogue*, which was about exhibitions and projects by the art schools of Yogyakarta and Jakarta. Around the same time, I was traveling to other cities with some friends to connect with art students.

In other words, the seed for ruangrupa had already been sown. We felt we were missing something, that we needed something, but didn't know what it was yet. In 1998 I transferred to the Rijksakademie in Amsterdam for two years. During that time we regularly wrote each other emails, which have unfortunately been lost. It would definitely be interesting to find and re-read our email correspondence. In any case, we stayed in touch during the months I was away. In 1998, the year of the Indonesian Reformarsi (Reformation), the widespread student movement brought about the overthrow of the regime that had been in power for 32 years. I learned about it in Amsterdam through activist friends who couldn't return at the time, and we took to the streets. Of course, these peaceful demonstrations in Amsterdam weren't comparable to the violent ones in Jakarta, where students got killed. By the way, the riots and massive violence are documented. When I met back up with friends after returning, we felt the need to formalize our meetings, discussions, and what we were doing. We wanted to start something, but what? We didn't call it a community or collective, but simply ruangrupa.

ruang means "space" and rupa means "visual" or "form". We put the two together to make "spaceform". We didn't actually have a space in the beginning though; we wanted a mental, non-physical one. We wanted to meet, gather, do projects, and research, show things and make them public. Everything gradually grew out of this need. We allied ourselves with organizations throughout the Global South as well as the Rijksakademie and the RAIN network; we moved into a small house and that's where we also worked. It was like the *ruruHaus*, except that we aren't supposed to sleep at the *ruruHaus*, although some of us do. The little house was a private domestic space where we initiated everything, between friends. ruangrupa was completely different from those alternative spaces and artist initiatives in Europe that used post-industrial spaces or large warehouses. Not just ruangrupa, but many other initiatives in Indonesia started in houses that were part of residential areas. That's why our vocabulary is also a domestic one from living spaces. We use words like living room, gathering, or hospitality because they fit well with our practice that was born out of the private, the public, the living, and the in-between. Everything is so entangled that you can't separate it. We're integrated into a neighborhood, and our projects and ideas are inspired by our existence, survival, and struggles in a city like Jakarta.

People often ask us where we get the ideas for our projects from. They come from life as an individual with its everyday problems. In 2003, we started holding a video festival every two years until 2017, one of the biggest in Southeast Asia, maybe even in all of Asia. We stopped it later because we got tired. We came up with the idea between 1998 and 2000, when the Internet and technology suddenly changed everything. We took advantage of it, like our friends were also doing, and said to ourselves, "Let's celebrate this technological elegance with festivals." From 2000 on, we organized a student forum every two years together with student friends, which is what we started out as. We wanted to do something in the middle of life, something about love, hate, and all that. If I'm not mistaken, *RURUKIDS* was the last edition of the forum we did because many of us now have children. I don't have any yet. Everything we realized in the 22 years is the result of individual and collective struggles. We saw with our own eyes how damn difficult it is to survive as artists who aren't market oriented and only work on a project basis. Without any public funding. Many friends were forced to do something else in order to survive, even though they were really talented. We developed *lumbung* to work against this. Since 2013, collaborating with other collectives has allowed our ideas to grow and evolve. As you can see, our collective develops out of what we see and experience.

NOT JUST RUANGRUPA, BUT MANY OTHER INITIATIVES IN INDONESIA STARTED IN HOUSES THAT WERE PART OF RESIDENTIAL AREAS. THAT’S WHY OUR VOCABULARY IS ALSO A DOMESTIC ONE FROM LIVING SPACES.

SECURING THE MINIMUM WAGE

TCE Speaking of *lumbung*, it's one of your key terms and originally refers to a rice barn. In your usage it becomes a place for sharing resources with others, a collective of collectives, and an economic model.

AD In Indonesia and other countries in the region, the art economy or market is limited, and we didn't learn that in art school. What does an artist do? Make artworks that they sell to survive, of course. That's what you get taught. But there are completely different ways of making art. What about the performance artists, video artists, media artists? We set out in that direction, and ruangrupa was lucky that we had access to various small sources of funding at the time: a little bit of public funding here, a little bit of international funding there, and also support from sponsors. Not many people had access to that kind of help. Around 2002 we received international funding from the Dutch organization Hivos for ten years. After 1998, after the reformation, a lot of NGOs set up shop with international support, to an extent unknown to previous generations, and the arts and culture sector as well as ruangrupa got a piece of the pie.

There was a lot of uncertainty since we knew that the windfall would be over in ten years, and that we didn't have the time or resources to experiment with other economic models. We had no idea how to continue. As far as I remember, we only had access to the funds for the next two years, so I suggested to the others that we use the two-year funds for something else, for experiments. They're going to stop the funding anyway, and when it dries up we'll be in a crisis. We didn't know what to expect. We would have a chance to continue if we could use the remaining two years of funding for experimentation to develop another model. Since the financial support was always project-based, it had to be used accordingly. But that wouldn't help us sustain the practice permanently. Maybe we could save some of it, but that also wouldn't get us anywhere in the long run. Many collectives faced the same situation we did. After the Dutch funders approved our proposal, we asked two or three other collectives, including Serrum and Grafis Huru Hara–whom we set up *Gudskul* (Contemporary Art Collective and Ecosystem Studies) with in 2018–what they thought about creating a joint business model offering artistic services, such as producing festivals, exhibitions, art management, art handling or design. The plan worked. We were able to raise between 20 and 25 percent of the money needed to finance our projects with it. That was around 2013, so the idea of *lumbung* was already laid out back then, in terms of how we pooled, maximized, and divided our resources. That was one factor; the other was space. As the rents got higher and higher, we asked other collectives how much they were paying in rent and if we shouldn't get together, rent a space together, and share it. Another factor: the situation of each individual in the collective. What about basic income and basic monetary needs? The members of the other collectives didn't have one; fortunately we had one for several years, but it was below the minimum wage. Together with the other collectives, we thought about what we could do to achieve this and build a practice that not only supports ideas but also individuals. Because without such support, the practice can't be sustained over a long period of time. This collective of collectives came out of that approach. We had to abandon the practice focussed on the single collective and expand it to include other *ekosistems* and partner with them to decentralize it. In 2015, we moved into a large space we called *Gudang Sarinah Ekosistem*. It's about 6,000 square meters, consisting of two units with 3,000 square meters each in a former warehouse. There's no living room. We did a lot there and started *lumbung* in everyday things, by sharing research space and equipment and doing various programs. Although we worked together for ten years and trusted each other, the last thing we did was to make the money transparent. It was strange. We took from others and also gave to others, ideas, space, everything. But no money. That only changed when the *lumbung* model started working, not only for collectives but also for individuals, so that everyone received a basic income. Now, more than sixty people active in *Gudskul* receive a monthly salary above the minimum wage. But we didn't see *lumbung* as something physical; we didn't just put extra money into some pot. It's not like that, it's just an idea or a value for us to practice transparency. I don't know how many bank accounts are floating around, but everything in this *Gudskul ekosistem* is transparent so that everything is available for everyone to see. We have a supervisory team that knows what is needed and what the surplus is, and also a regular meeting.

SECRET LIFE UNDER THE REGIME

TCE What was it like when you organized your first music festivals in the era of the dictatorship?

AD They happened underground on a small scale, so word didn't get out. I don't remember any violence. But whenever we started talking about power, corruption, and the ruling party of the time, there was immediate censorship and self-censorship. To this day, corruption and authority are still important issues that I'm concerned with and talk about. Since the very beginning, officially establishing an organization or group in Indonesia has always been a big deal. We've learned this under various power relations, both in the era of Dutch colonization and the period of independence. Authorities always see gatherings as a threat. And we love to communicate; there's always a debate about how we can gather as citizens, whether publicly or privately. During the Suharto regime, any form of gathering or group organizing without official permission was a subversive act. You could get caught and arrested. Although the law was fundamentally revised after 1998, to this day people still get critical looks when they assemble.

TCE Did the external circumstances, especially the political ones, bring you closer as a group? Did they also play a role in the development of *lumbung*?

AD Yes, I mean, the 90s generation was traumatized by the regime, and I think that we're unconsciously trying to mock and destroy this construct. Even when we know we won't succeed, we still have to try to deconstruct it, and that becomes increasingly difficult after all the years.

Today, we're working with a younger generation, with friends who are 20 to 25 years younger than me. They didn't experience the Suharto regime or its downfall, and they live under different power relations. I think one reason for *Gudskul* is definitely that this educational platform allows us to implement and communicate the ideas in a critical way. I think the younger people have their own politics, which are also very different because the art scene has changed a lot and the power relations are structured differently.

During the regime, it was all vertical. You had the military, police, and other agencies that oppressed the people. Today, control operates more horizontally. Before 1998, censorship came from the state; after 1998, it came from neighbors who held different beliefs, such as religious ones. In a way, we have to take this into account in our practice. There are a lot of problems in the education system. Instead of just opposing, we said, "Okay, we won't complain. Let's do it better!"

TCE Your practice of *Gudskul* seems as if in your eyes the current system is not the right one and that you want to develop other models of living together. Perhaps building a better world wasn't your goal at first, but the worldwide network of different collectives that you are building could actually change the world.

AD Yes, definitely. The more everything grew and the deeper we went, the more we understood how and where everything is rooted. Everything is rooted in our perception of the world, as well as in how we imagine living together. It isn't just about knowledge, but also how we act today, how we perceive art, power, and economics. Neither so-called institutional critique nor art in general is enough to comprehend all the complexity and change something. By just resisting the way things are and criticizing the art and education that come from the old values, we lose the strength and time for our own ways, our own experiments, and reflecting on how something new can emerge, how we can create better values. And that can't be done without experimenting with economics as one of the foundations. Economics determine the basis of how we live with each other. You can't change one without the other.

TCE You've invited many collectives from different cultures to documenta fifteen. Do the cultural differences make it difficult to integrate them into your global network? And how do you manage such a large system? How do you keep track of everything?

AD Yes, the challenges are also because there are different cosmologies, different ways of seeing oneself, of practicing things, of believing in oneself. And work as well as the relationships between society and the individual are different. But that's what makes it exciting. We're not interested in having others illustrate or adopt our ideas, rather we want to learn from other models, because that way we involve many more people. We're thinking long-term. It's more about passion than looking for one single solution. You all know what a trap exhibition making can be. It was clear to us from the beginning that it wouldn't be easy and that we would be colliding with a lot of different models and approaches. And then we saw how diverse and different these models are, how rich local contexts are. What does contemporary art mean in a place like Haiti or a rural region? Wherever I traveled, I learned about art. Both in Jakarta and in Amsterdam. ruangrupa also learned a lot by leaving our education and cosmological context behind. In the context of ruangrupa's global network, we aren't trying to present *lumbung* as a solution. It would be a trap to even try. It's about building bridges between the different struggles and local contexts, learning from each other, and recognizing that we all suffer from this coercive system of conformity and assimilation.

THE INDONESIAN PATH TO INDEPENDENCE

TCE Do your openness to collaborating with collectives from other cultures and your idea of globalization also relate to the question of colonization and Indonesia's specific history?

AD That's a hard question to answer. We won. There aren't many countries that overcame colonization through their own battles and revolutions. We proclaimed our independence in 1945, not 1949 as the Dutch claim, because the war of independence was already being waged everywhere in Indonesia between 1945 and 1949. At the outset of the 20th century, there were a lot of youth organizations on the different islands of Indonesia. They went to school, got smarter, and started organizing themselves. Indonesia as a concept, as a country or nation emerged in the 1920s when young people and students held mass anti-colonial demonstrations. Back then, there wasn't any Indonesia in the contemporary sense–it was more like an agreement within the independence movement that was consolidating at the time. People knew that the only way to become independent and liberate themselves from the colonizers was to unite.

The recurring question of why collectivism and a sense of community is so pronounced in Indonesia could possibly be answered by looking back at this history. Talk of being united to free oneself from colonial powers has become national propaganda by now; at the time, it worked. You can argue about it, of course, but there were a lot of people from the nationalist movement of the time for whom independence from the colonizers meant being educated, Western, and modern. You know, when you're on the same level as the colonial masters, that's when you're fighting, and that's exactly what happened back then. Though the question is whether that approach is still relevant, since that kind of model produces a lot of exploitation and suffering. *lumbung* is nothing new. It's more like returning to the past than finding something new. The practice is even pre-modern, and that's interesting.

TCE Did *Gudskul* also come from a distrust of institutions?

AD Yes, there are several important points. I mentioned earlier that we see *Gudskul* as a way to critically shape or regenerate collective practice. I also think that institutions everywhere are very slow and irrelevant, mainly because of their size and bureaucracy. So there is still a certain space where institutions are touched by the reality outside their walls. That's why we call it the *ekosistem*. As I mentioned earlier, our practice is very closely connected to and rooted in life.

Back when we were students, we also lived in the art school. Later on in the 1970s, the university was neutralized and depoliticized because of the potential danger posed by it and the students who gathered there. In 1997, the campus of my art school in Yogyarta, which was previously in the middle of a residential area, was geographically pushed out of the city and moved to a large piece of land where there was nothing, and that's where the new art school was built.

It was a systematic act motivated by the fear of unrest, and we tried to reverse it so that living together, working together, and urban life could be reunited. Everything has changed enormously. In my brother's generation, we could still study for nine or ten years. Today you have to finish in four and a half or five years. If you don't make it, you drop out.

When we founded ruangrupa, we wrote a critique of the way art and cultural institutions operated, which was very institutionalized, bureaucratic, not exactly open, let alone organic. And we also thought that the art market in 2000 was more production and object-based, rather than a research-oriented process. Thinking about the text from back then now, I have to laugh as things have only gotten worse. Today Jakarta has more institutionalized museums and two art fairs, back then there wasn't even one. We drew our conclusion and decided to offer other options.

OVERCOMING POWER STRUCTURES

TCE What is your experience with documenta in Kassel, with bringing in your ideas, your background, and context, and creating an atmospheric force that takes people somewhere they couldn't have imagined before?

AD We're trying to change a lot of relationships, including power structures. The art world–made up of curators, artists, organizers and collectors–is problematic insofar as it is subject to power structures that determine how the art is made. That's why we're trying to forge new relationships. It isn't something you can do overnight. It's also risky because, like it or not, you have to open the documenta on June 18 and do the events for the public to experience. That's also why we planned from the beginning to mix this with the *ruruHaus*, to experience it together with the visitors. We don't know what it will be like yet. It's an experiment. The documenta may not have the time we need, but there is a certain amount of time to prepare. I don't think the model we designed for Kassel could be transferred to a biennial. The duration would be too short. It could be applied to a museum since it also has the privilege of time. I think it's also important for an exhibition or event like documenta to be able to think beyond itself. It isn't didactic; it's more regenerative, not only in practice but also in thinking. There isn't a single event where we thought it's only about the event itself. That's a very egocentric model, extremely extractive, limited to a specific time, defined for a collective purpose in a specific space, and also very bowdlerizing. We don't want to think of documenta as the end or a single thing. We still have a lot ahead of us.

TCE You aren't striving for a sudden revolution, but an evolution, by bringing together disparate collectives from all over the world into a network, so that everywhere in the world, in every country and on every continent, small collective islands emerge where people are already practicing a different form of coexistence. And as time goes by, there'll be more and more, and one day the world might have become a different place because of it.

AD Yes, I like how you put it. Scale is important here. It's like a rhizome that needs a mechanism or model to organize itself and divide like a cell. I once wrote about these small and medium-sized initiatives. We never think of it as something big, but rather, as you say, an ensemble of islands small, medium, and many.

TCE Like the Indonesian islands.

AD Exactly. The challenge is to make sure they're connected, talking to each other, learning from each other.

TCE Yes, that's beautiful. It's close to where you started out. You started in living rooms, so you weren't centralized. And now, with the globalization brought about by the internet, you can develop even more on the outside and understand the dimensions behind the system. The system is adaptive in some sense; it's not like creating a single system, then spreading it everywhere. No monopolization.

AD Exactly.

TCE And each system learns from the other, and we're also learning from you as a result of doing this research. What remains of what you've done in the places where you've worked?

AD What's important to us is whether we made friendship out of it.

TCE What does friendship mean to you?

AD That we have conversations, stay in touch, hang out together, help each other, and trust each other. A project is more like a tool for friendship, and that's part of our values. It's a word that's easily misused. Maybe it sounds corny, too. And we're also traumatized in relation to the word, insofar as we suffered a lot during the Suharto regime because of friendships in the form of nepotism. When playing, hanging out, cooking together, there are also many interpersonal relationships and power relations that we're always consciously and unconsciously trying to parody and break with.

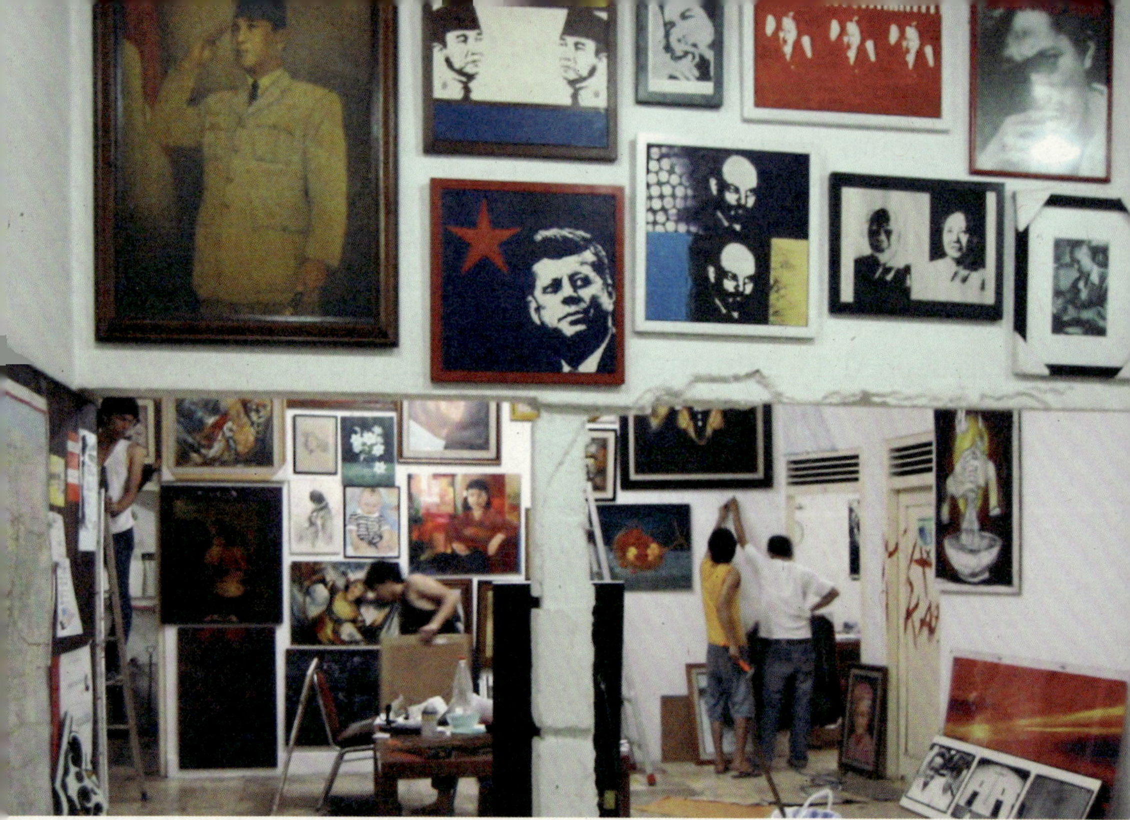

Garbage Sale, 2003

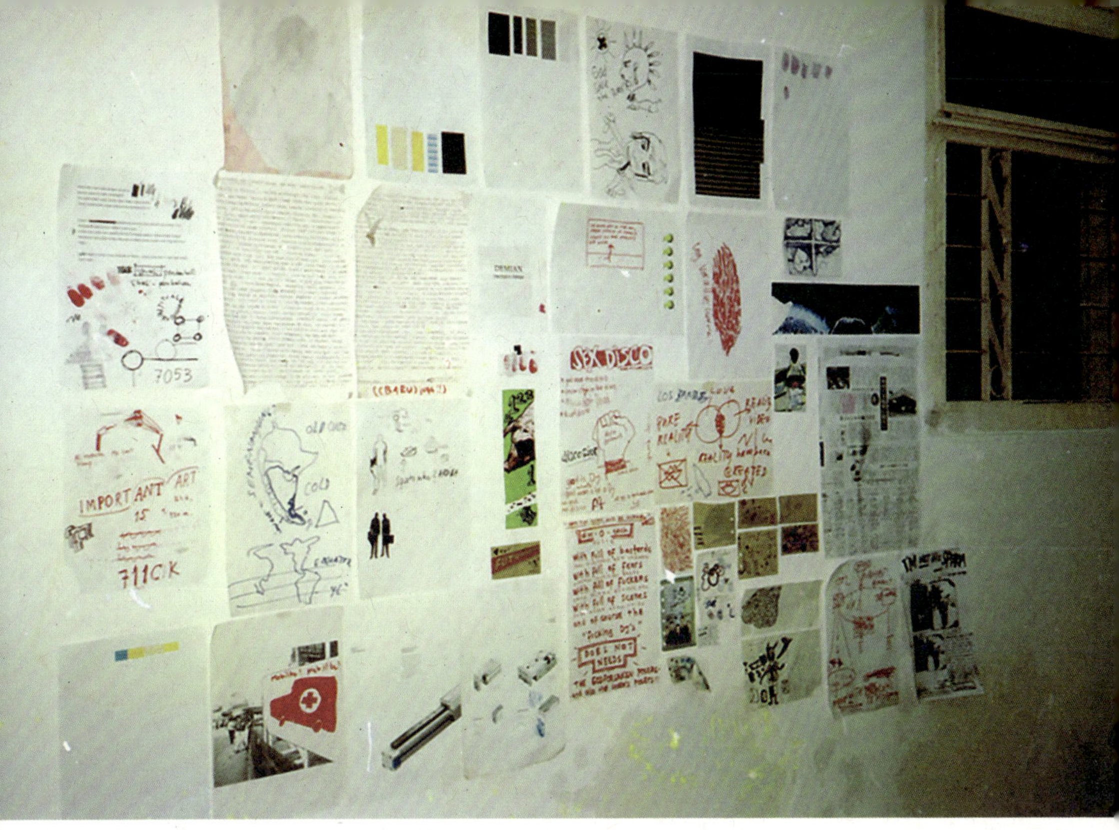

ruangrupa's studio, 2003

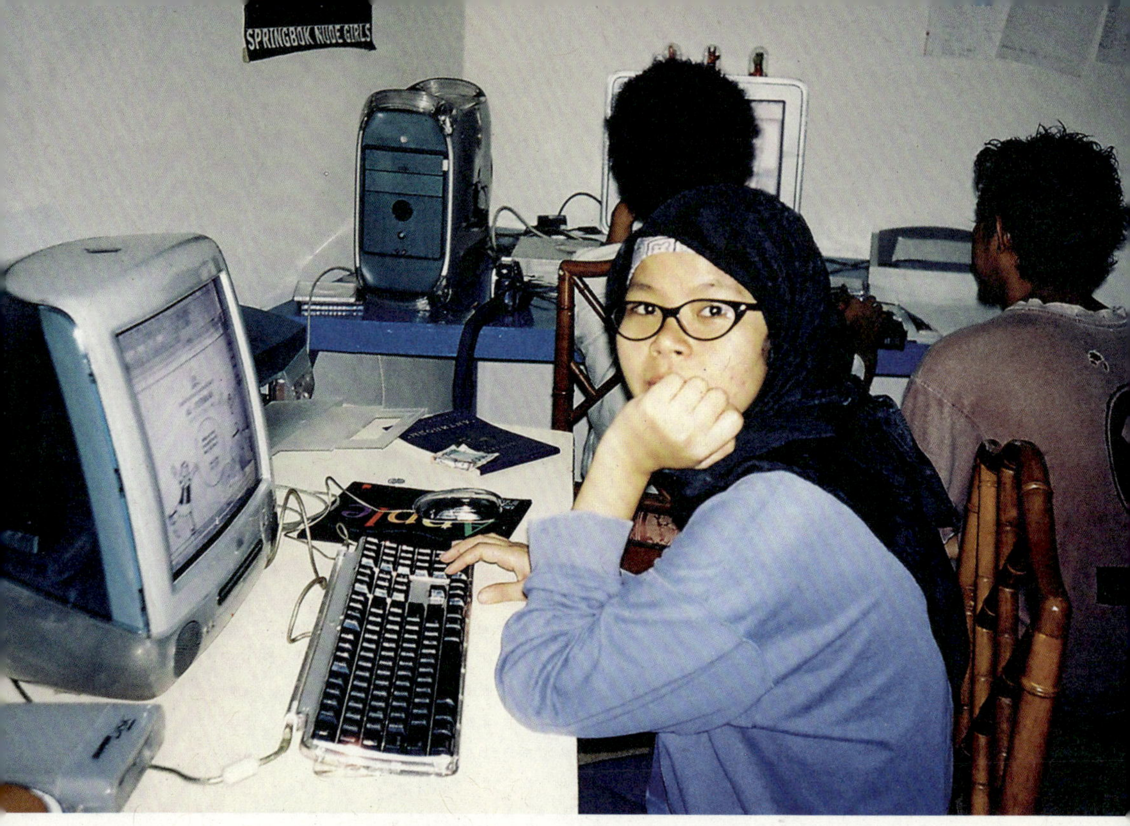

Daniella Kunil, Anggun Priambodo, Ade Darmawan, 2001

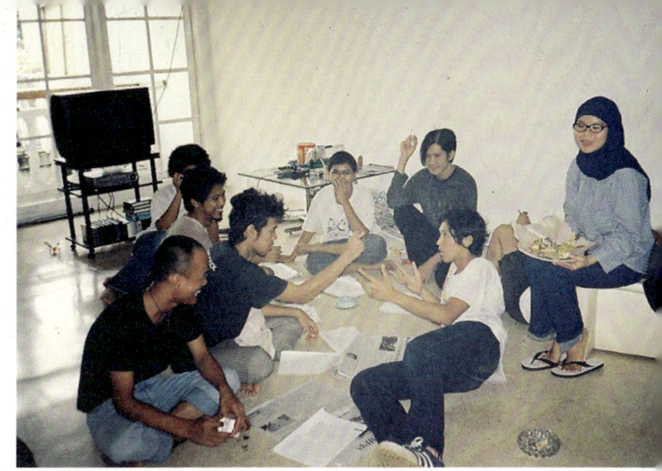

Meeting of ruangrupa, 2001

ruangrupa's studio, 2001

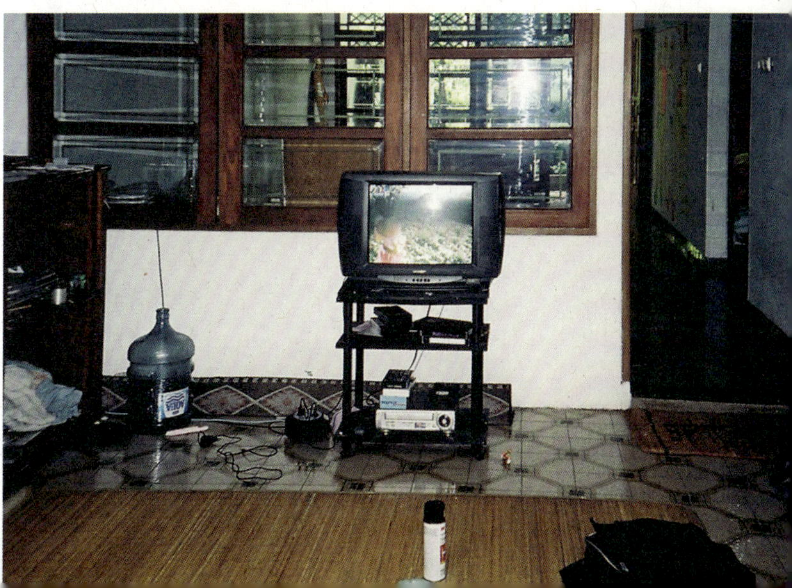

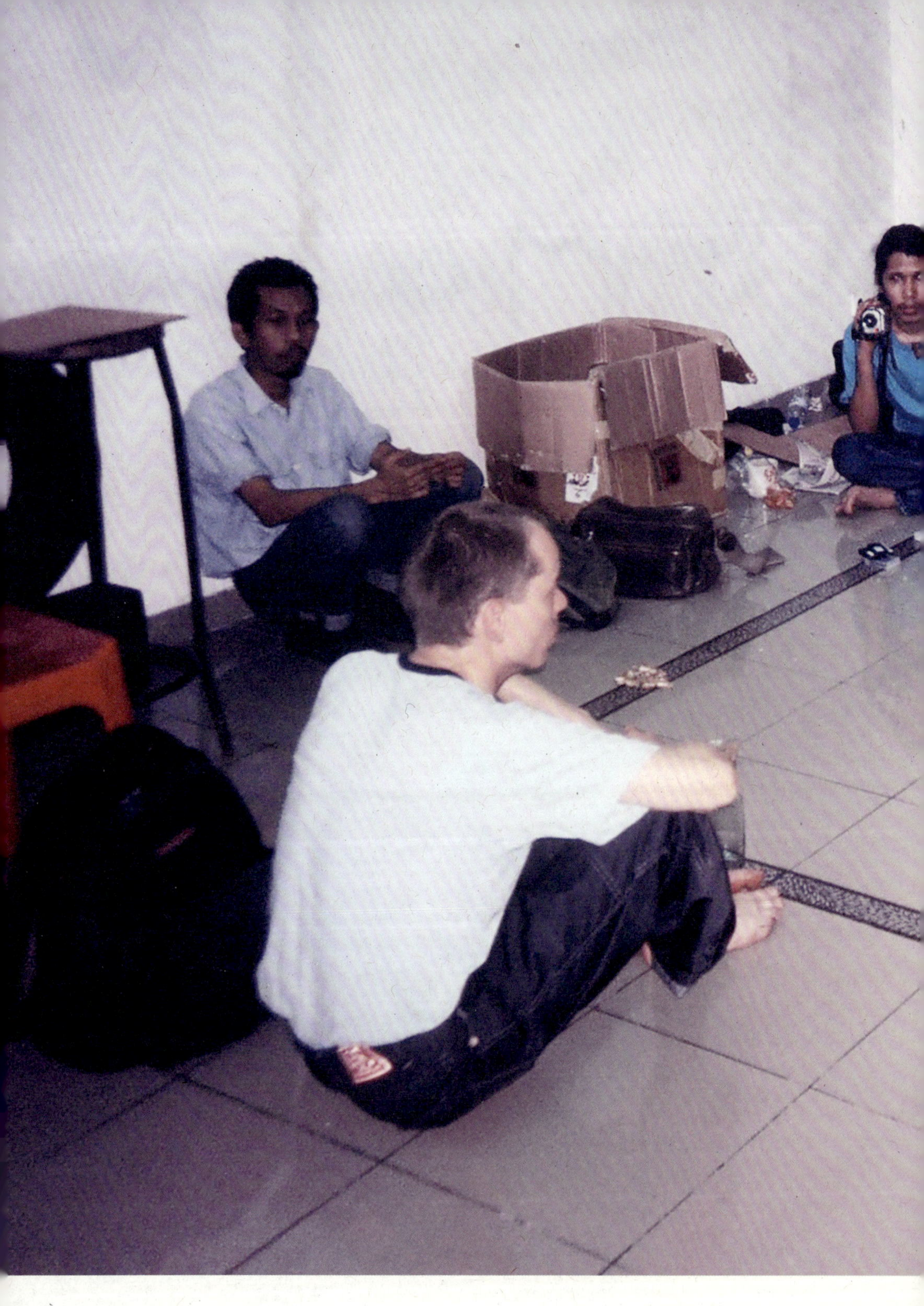

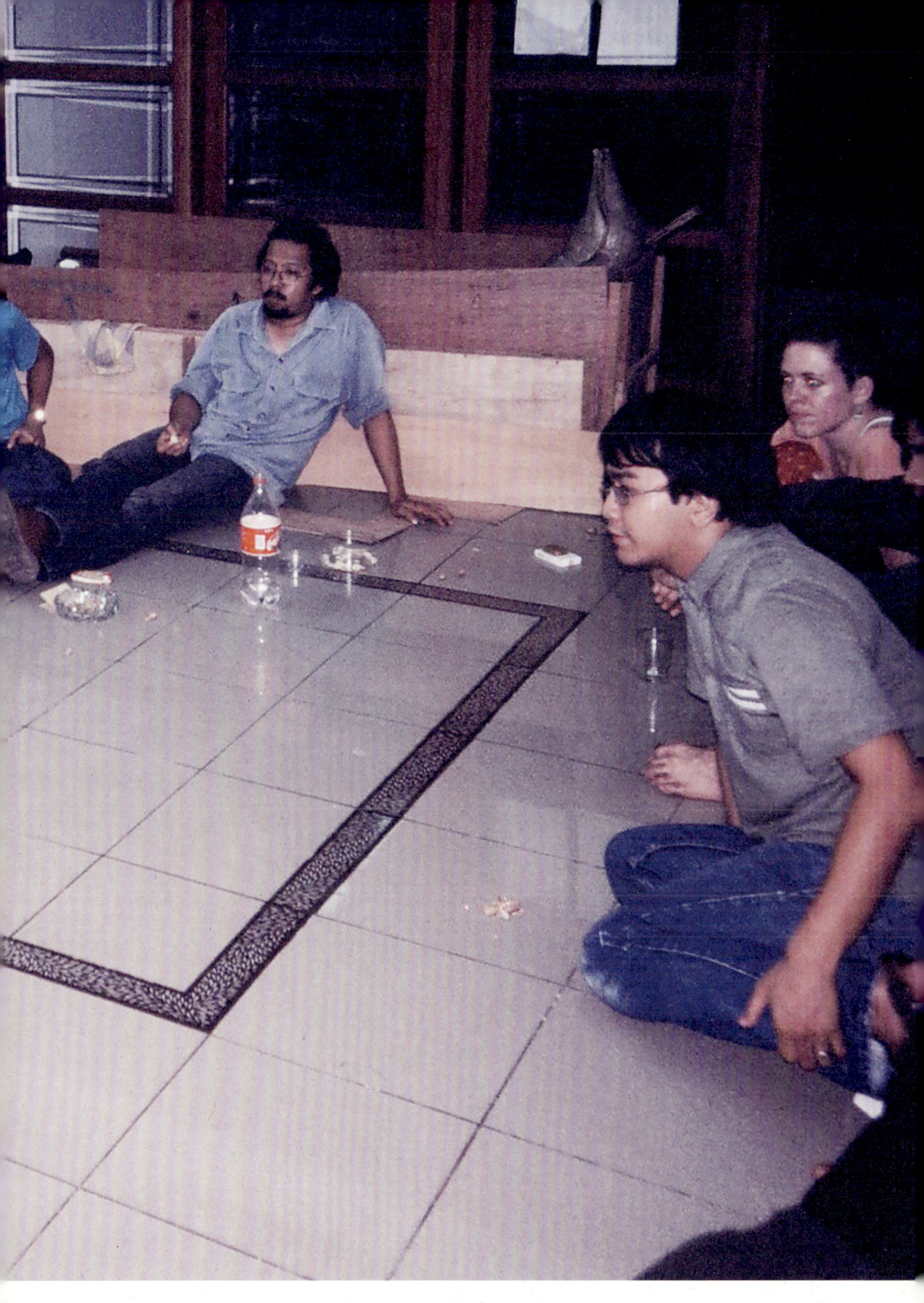

Presentation of the *Swarm Projects*, 2001

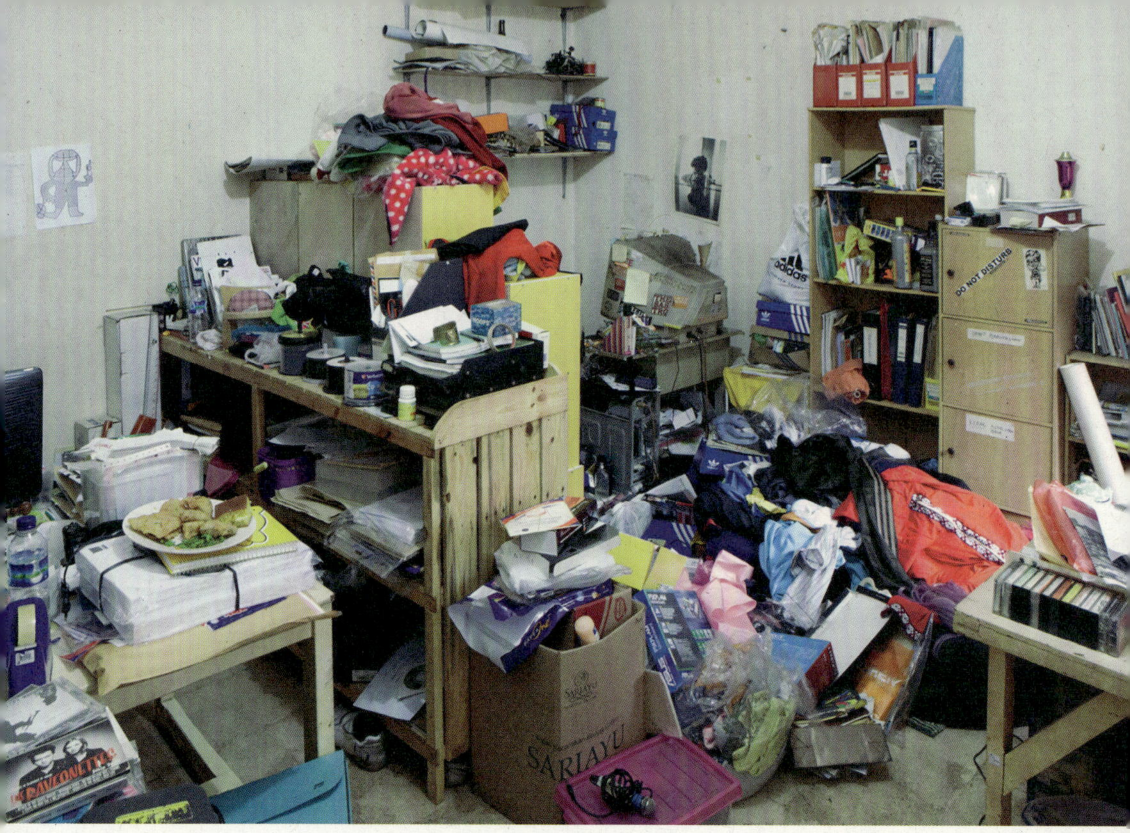

ruangrupa's first studio, 2001

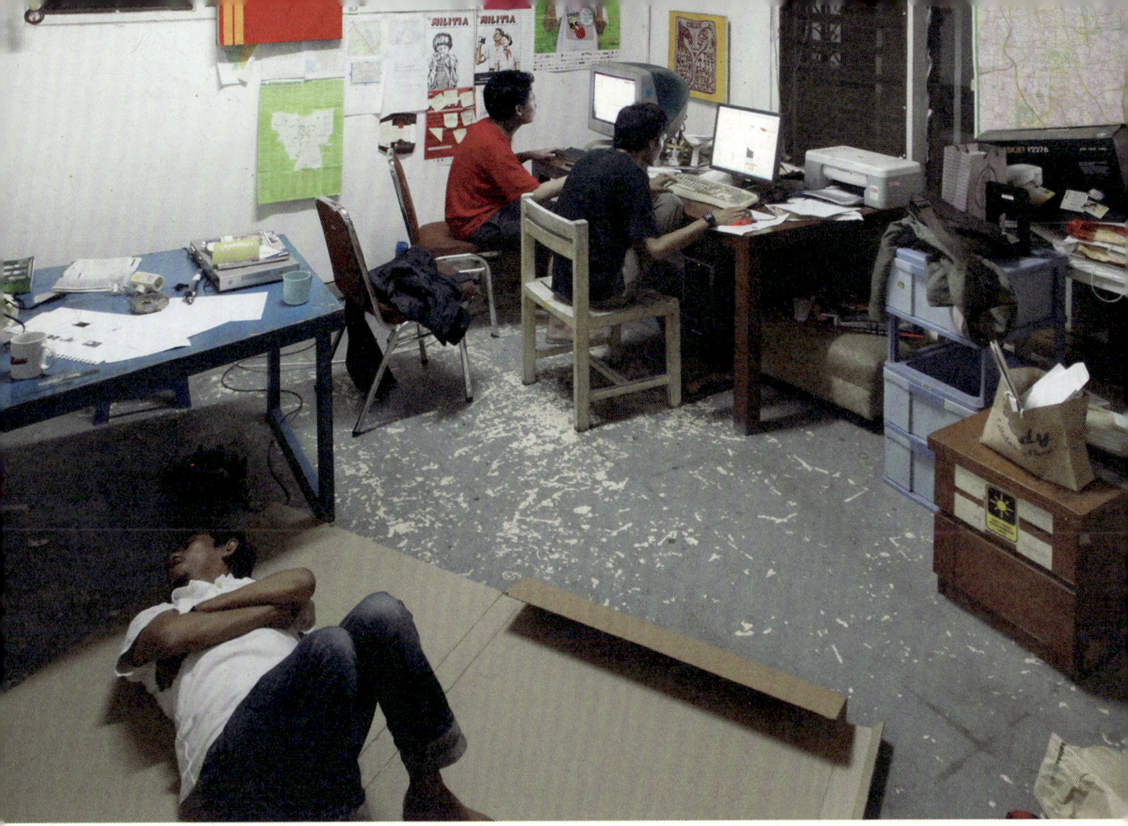

Working, hanging out and living: at ruangrupa there are no boundaries between art and everyday life.

THE COLLECTIVE AND PUNK

IN CONVERSATION WITH FARID RAKUN

TCE How did it all start for you?

FR I think even before the happy years after the fall of Suharto's New Order regime in May 1998, Reza, Ameng, and Ade were friends. Reza and Ameng studied at the Jakarta Art Institute, Ade in Yogyakarta at the Indonesian Art Institute. Anyway, they knew each other from events like underground hardcore metal concerts and met regularly to talk about the art scene. Still in 1998, a year after his first solo exhibition at Cemeti Contemporary Art Gallery in Yogyakarta, Ade transferred to the Rijksakademie in Amsterdam, which didn't stop him from starting the group at the same time. This turned into ruangrupa in 2000. I learnt about them around 2003. I liked their particular way of approaching urban themes. It made me curious. Their reflections on urbanism were completely different from those at the architecture school where I was studying. I started hanging out with ruangrupa every now and then, but eventually it became more regular. It was a good place to get drunk before we went clubbing at night, as many spaces of collective practice in Indonesia were doing at the time. Joining ruangrupa didn't have anything to do with my professional aspirations, or even with wanting to educate myself intellectually and strengthen my cognitive awareness. I just felt comfortable in their company. I think I made ruangrupa my imaginary client and also used them as an architecture student. That's how it all started for me.

TCE It sounds like an organic development, as though ruangrupa's founding was primarily based on friendship, a shared mindset, and a shared interest in art, architecture, and urban development. In other words, friendship and hanging out together were the deciding factors for you to initiate joint projects, right?

FR It's like you say. The individual stories are different. Everyone had their own special moment of choosing or deciding to join ruangrupa. For me, it came after I graduated from highschool. I had left Jakarta, moved first to Bali, and then to Phnom Penh. I had to get out of Jakarta. It isn't an easy place to live, not one for the faint of heart. A lot of things come together there: traffic jams, pollution, high prices. All of this is a real problem. Living in Bali is considerably cheaper than Jakarta. While I was away, I stayed in sporadic contact with ruangrupa. When I returned in 2010, they needed editorial help for their online journal, Karbon Journal, which focuses on the problems of public space and urban visual culture in Indonesia. And since I'd decided to stop working as a professional architect–it was too administrative, risk averse, and not creative enough for me–one of several options was to become one of their editors. Starting with editing and commissioning, I became more involved as time went on. In between, I still worked on architectural and art projects. From 2011 to 2013, I temporarily left Jakarta one more time, but knowing that I would return and spend more time with ruangrupa after my studies. I felt like getting more involved. Like I said, it was friendship that bound us together, combined with the pleasure of being together. During the time spent together, we thought up strategies. How can we make ruangrupa sustainable for individuals and deal with the financial burden that ruangrupa has to bear?

At the moment, I'm focusing on documenta fifteen one hundred percent. It isn't always easy to keep a balance between the need to make a living and collective work, since a collective isn't exactly the optimal way to make money. Each of us chose their own way, their strategy to survive financially and make their contribution to ruangrupa.

CELEBRATING THE REGIME'S DOWNFALL

TCE How was it even possible for you to organize music festivals during the dictatorship?

FR To this day, the poor suburbs of Jakarta, Tangerang, and Bekasi are strongholds of punk. Despite censorship, and even though the regime prohibited everything that threatened or diminished its power, concerts were possible because there were still niches and they happened underground. The regime rigorously cracked down on anything that it didn't feel comfortable with. Groups were broken up as soon as more than five people who weren't part of the same family gathered under one roof. They were arrested, interrogated, and ended up who knows where. Universities and schools were seen as hotbeds of political activity, and the student body actually proved to be the most powerful force of protest in 1998. They were the ones who called out for demonstrations most of all. Today's students are wired quite differently than we were back then. The situation and climate at the universities have shifted considerably, and since 1998 the state has been much more adept at dealing with students.

Because there was enormous pressure on us, because meetings and gatherings of any kind were forbidden, and because anything that displeased the regime risked danger, the fall of the New Order was greeted with jubilation and great relief. And people celebrated accordingly. The sudden release of tension was like steam escaping from a high-pressure boiler. Not only in the field of art, but also in other areas, collectives of various kinds mushroomed. Even fishermen, farmers, and religious movements joined together to form groups. Under Suharto, religion was one of the most controlled fields. So were the arts, especially theater and literature, from which the greatest dissent emanated.

TCE Wasn't organizing musical events dangerous?

FR No, not really. We were lucky that the powers-that-be weren't really interested in small or niche events like punk concerts at the time. From that point of view, there was no self-censorship. It's true that it wasn't possible to discuss communism, and we couldn't openly debate LGBTQIA+ issues and all that, but there were loopholes in the system that we used to get around the bans and censorship. At the Jakarta Biennale, at events that we did, at all these things, we never had any serious problems; there wasn't any government interference. They never moved against us, nor did we get any support. We weren't personally hindered or in our activities, which was fine for us; everything was manageable.

TCE Weren't you under surveillance?

FR Of course we were under surveillance. There were spies on site watching what we did. Anyone who grew up in that time knows how to recognize spies and civilian policemen. Usually they left us alone. What we were doing seemed too small and meaningless to them; it wasn't going anywhere as far as they were concerned. But maybe what I'm saying is too speculative.

And, of course, these kinds of events were also druggy. From the 1990s to the mid-2000s, drugs were ubiquitous, especially in Jakarta, and I lost a lot of friends to drugs. I think drugs also served as a kind of weapon that they allowed, if not supported, in order to get rid of a whole generation. Consumption wasn't controlled back then, unlike nowadays, when drugs are strictly forbidden, there's a big anti-drug campaign, and it's hard to get them.

TCE In 1998, after the regime fell, everything in Jakarta was open, and it still wasn't clear where society's collective journey was headed. Did the strong need to form collectives also have to do with the fact that it was unclear what would happen next?

FR Yes, that's how it was in Yogyakarta, Bandung, and a lot of other places.

TCE What was the atmosphere like?

FR Optimistic, full of hope and confidence. After the dictatorship, there was a big sigh of relief and the feeling that we could finally do what we wanted and be free. We finally had opportunities that we had been deprived of before, despite the economic situation, which was shitty. It was the Asian crisis, and it took ten years to rebuild everything. Even though the economy was in shambles, there was a positive atmosphere, both politically and culturally. This was also reflected in the state's apologies to those who had suffered oppression and persecution under the dictatorship, like the Chinese, for example, whom a lot of terrible things had happened to. Their vehicles and stores in Medan had been set on fire by rioters; they were harassed and excluded as a minority. All in all, there was a cheerful spirit of optimism, a better atmosphere than today, despite the depressing economic conditions.

THE JOY OF BELONGING TOGETHER

TCE You speak about that time with the word "we." When exactly was the moment of "Okay, we're going to work as a collective?" Was the desire to participate in shaping society's future one of the motivations for creating ruangrupa?

FR I think it started with that interest. Moreover, we were punks, right, so we were against the establishment and all that stuff. Coming together was one thing. The second was the fact that without getting together, we didn't have access to certain things. We became ruangrupa and many other collectives formed alongside us because we all realized that we are stronger united and can achieve more as a group than as isolated individuals. Through the student movement's success, we also experienced a sense of belonging, the joy of belonging, and the benefits of being a collective. When subjected to a failed state, one that continues failing to this day, caring for each other was essential for survival. The solidarity was and still is great today. For us in Indonesia, it's easy and nothing unusual to form a collective; we know it from our families. We learned to be there for each other from an early age and that we shouldn't primarily just think about ourselves. You know, it doesn't matter how brilliant you are if you're only useful to yourself. It's just that the extent differs from family to family. In any case, self-centeredness is strange to us. Generally, I think that because of the state's total failure, the safety net was in families and neighborhoods. The collective sensibility grew out of that. Here in Indonesia, it matured into a hotbed of art collectives. More research is needed to understand where the drive toward collectivity comes from. We knew that our interests weren't taken seriously by power, the market, galleries, and museums. That got us thinking about how to create our own space. Since most of us were born in Jakarta, a global metropolis, we knew from the start that we had to be global too. Networks, which were called South-South networks back then, were extremely important in establishing contacts with people from Argentina, Brazil, Mali, Turkey, and so on. Back in 2001, we set up residencies with the intention of establishing and maintaining friendships beyond Jakarta and Indonesia. We did it on a whim. We only figure out what we're doing and why in retrospect. We learn from it in retrospect, not while we're doing it. If you had asked me the same questions in 2000, you'd probably gotten completely different answers.

TCE How did you get into punk? You've emphasized that punk is anti-establishment. Punk seems to not only have shaped your thinking. Did it also influence how you think about art, how you work and operate without running the risk of becoming established and thus losing yourself?

FR You should ask Reza this question. I'd be curious to hear his answer. Like other teenagers, I got into punk in highschool, in the time before Spotify. You know how teenagers are prone to angst, and it also took hold of me, so I read up on the history of the music. Punk is about the sound, the attitude, about people disconnected and excluded from society, and the underground situation.

The fact that punk appealed to us is probably related to the fact that most of us felt rejected by the industry, if not society, in one way or another, and we knew that the collective was a good way to protect our interests, secure our lives, and not lose our minds in the process. Yes, the music was extremely important. Every one of us was active in the scene or made music. Some of us took it further. It wasn't just about punk aesthetics, but also about supporting local music movements. We're still involved to this day.

TCE Is there a difference between the Western and Indonesian understanding of punk?

FR Yes, definitely. Punk in Indonesia is very specific, which might be one reason why Indonesia is still a vibrant hotspot of heavy metal today. Also the way of understanding Islam is different, though it is comparable. We aren't unique in anything. We drew on a global subcultural phenomenon but kept twisting it until it became part of our culture or something of our own. Like we tended to punk then, younger people are drawn to hip-hop now. For a relatively short period, between 2000 and 2010, the club scene was the place that opened up those opportunities for me. Probably not in the same way today, or at least not in Jakarta. Being a punk in Indonesia is certainly different was fashionable in the Western hemisphere. Just five years ago, punks in Aceh, an Indonesian province on the northwestern tip of Sumatra, were being harassed by police because of their appearance.

TCE Where does your anti-establishment approach come from? From your experience with the dictatorship?

FR That's certainly one aspect, but it can't be reduced to that alone. It also has to do with the presidential elections, the Indonesian art scene, the market, the gallery scene. It was always a mystery to us how one could operate in these constellations under their conditions. The older we got, the more we understood how politics, the state, the institutions, the country, and the city function. In that context, our saving grace was recognizing that always just being antagonistic and against the system doesn't get us anywhere. We criticize by doing something different. We couldn't find a space, so we opened one. We didn't have a market, so we created one. That's how we learned to do things.

TCE Is punk still something that unites you? Are your activities and the creation of your own space also punk? Is being anti the basis of your togetherness?

FR I am glad that you associate ruangrupa with punk. As I said, after 2016 we realized that just being against something doesn't get us anywhere. If we didn't mature in our approach, something would be wrong with us. Together with the collectives Serrum and Grafis Huru Hara, we set up the informal educational platform *Gudskul* in 2018. We realized that although collectivity is one of the most important practices for artists in Indonesia, it isn't included in any school curricula, so we set up our own. I'm not trying to say that what gets taught in the official schools is wrong; ours is more complementary. You can't learn things like collective work in school, but you can with us. Our *ekosistem* is holistic and includes many different collaborators: artists, curators, art writers, managers, researchers, musicians, filmmakers, architects, chefs, designers, and street artists.

TCE Even before documenta, you were working outside of Indonesia. What were your experiences like in countries with different mentalities, cultures, and market structures?

FR It never gets easier. We tend not to impose our ideas and what we have on others. A collective is one way of doing things differently, and certainly not the only one. We ourselves have learned from exchanges with others and experienced how some of our ideas and sensibilities are received in different contexts, not only in Europe, but also in Japan, South Korea, and Singapore.

TCE What is it like for you not to work in Kassel because of Covid-19, but to work on documenta fifteen from Jakarta?

FR I can't estimate how present or influential it is or what people in Kassel and Germany are thinking or saying about what we do for documenta. That's beyond my knowledge. But we've already had our experiences elsewhere with what we're doing. After all, visitors to Kassel aren't going to experience something we just started doing yesterday. Of course, the output isn't exactly the same. There are differences here and there. The skills, the modalities, and the strategies are different, but the core isn't. Why's it on everyone's lips now? Let's just say it's gotten louder. From our biased perspective, it seems kind of strange. Against that background, the feedback, the impressions, and reactions of others are exciting for us. The fact that we're now getting this kind of attention is probably also due to our development. In 2007, biennial circuit started noticing us, and after riding that wave for a while, we became the curators of *SONSBEEK '16: transACTION* in Arnhem in 2016. To have arrived where we are today is either luck or fate.

WE WERE DEBUTANTS

TCE Back to your beginnings, how did you become known as ruangrupa in Indonesia in the first place?

FR We got attention for the events that we were actually doing for ourselves. The Indonesian art scene hasn't understood that until today (laughs). The fact that we're curating documenta fifteen solidified their understanding of ruangrupa as artists who organize events and set up platforms instead of making artworks. They include the music and video art festival, the student forum, the karaoke sessions, and also our radio station. That's been kind of refreshing. Sometimes we get asked where the visual art is in what we do. For us, that's the wrong question because it's foreign to us to make distinctions between visual and sound art, design and architecture. Since we're many people with different interests, passions, and preferences, we're accordingly open to all disciplines and media. We pursue everything and create something of our own from it. We build worlds.

TCE Why did you start a video festival?

FR Because many of us started playing with the medium in 2002, as music video directors, video artists, video or short film makers. We didn't have much knowledge at the time. We were debutants and wanted to get more involved with video. We created the festival because it gave us the opportunity to invite people we thought were exciting and whom we could learn more about the medium from. Of course, there were video artists in Indonesia at the time. But since they were older than us and belonged to a different generation, their works and their way of talking about them didn't appeal to us much. Anyway, around 2003 people started recording video clips, and one issue that occupied us was how to deal with porn, which was illegal in Indonesia and still is, by the way, even though there is a lot of amateur porn circulating in various channels. The Internet has changed and accelerated all these things. And there was the national television station, also a developing culture a culture of video games. There was a lack of information about all of this, and in that context a video festival certainly made a lot of sense. On that note, maybe one more anecdote: the art schools, which claimed to be the gatekeepers of art and video in Indonesia, had a hard time with our approach and expressed their displeasure in a friendly Indonesian way.

TCE What did the *Ok. Video – Jakarta International Video Art Festival* teach you?

FR Besides the content, that we no longer had a problem with not being popular with everyone. How we can position ourselves more clearly. How the New Order used new media to assert its interests and secure its power. They were quicker than artists and media activists to recognize the benefits. If I'm not mistaken, we took up the topic of the New Order in 2015. We understood the importance of establishing an international festival. We later lifted the initial restriction of only video. We expanded it to include new media. The biggest gain that came out of being involved with video was knowing how to work, co-govern, manage, and how an institution can get in our way.

TCE What was the composition of the audience?

FR The newness of video art was reflected in the youthfulness of the audience, ranging from highschool students to first-year university students. I was also a student at the time. Many of those who graduated a long time ago and are now in their late 30s or early 40s are still with us, for example as listeners of the radio station. As for the music festivals, we still care about them; we want to support the people who helped us.

TCE Do the experiences gained from video festivals have an impact on collective practice, even when dealing with a major event like documenta?

FR Yes, very much so. In 2017, we stopped hosting the *Ok. Video – Jakarta International Video Art Festival*. In terms of scale and changing an institution, documenta fifteen is the first, and hopefully not the last, time that we've put all our ambition and energy into making it as optimal as possible. Since it isn't taught at any school in Jakarta, we are teaching ourselves how to curate, step by step. Of course, we know about the myth of the curator and all these things. How we make decisions has changed over the years, and we've learned from our mistakes. With the 2007 *Ok. Video – Jakarta International Video Art Festival*, to pick just one example, the plan was to have it tour thirteen cities in Indonesia. The price we paid was that a lot of us ended up hating each other. We argued fiercely and almost broke up. Learning from that, we experimented with what we now know as *lumbung*, collectives that make assemblies, between 2016 and 2018. In the process, we were influenced by other networks that were part of collaborative assemblies, as well as by other approaches and ways of decision making. So documenta fifteen is the culmination of many things, and not just ours, but the work of many other collectives and artists. We're learning a lot, and not only from the path ruangrupa took. We're also drawing on others' knowledge of how to organize things and communicate with institutions.

THE MAGIC OF THE COLLECTIVE

TCE Listening to you, my impression is that there's a difference between Indonesian and European collectives. In Europe, as soon as an artist in the collective senses a chance to succeed as an individual, they leave the group. Against this background, it seems almost magical to me that you stayed together.

FR I don't know if that's magic. It isn't quite as smooth as it seems. I don't want to demystify it completely, but the fact is that many friends have come and gone in the past twenty years. It didn't always go as harmoniously as you're suggesting. If you were to ask people from the Indonesian art scene for their opinion of ruangrupa or about their personal experiences with us, the verdict or stance wouldn't be unanimously positive. The fact that we stick together like this and manage to keep patching things up is partly due to the fact that we deal with conflicts openly and don't avoid them. We've also known each other so well for so long that we know what makes the other person tick. A lot of things remain unsaid between us, but we understand each other, which is why we've been lucky so far. The Western art scene is different from the Indonesian art scene in that the temptation to be co-opted by the establishment, the market, the state, or institutions has only been limited so far. It isn't cooler and it doesn't make you richer or more powerful if you produce for the market, if you work for the national gallery, the ministry, or commercial galleries. Some of us who took this path have returned, others haven't. We aren't stopping anyone or criticizing this move. Some have left ruangrupa to work as curators or designers at MACAN, the first private museum of a collector of contemporary and modern art in Indonesia. That's fine and even good, because it enriches our knowledge as long as we keep talking to each other. It's knowledge that someone like me might never use, that I might never have access to. I could never work for a ministry. Sitting in an office from nine in the morning until five in the evening and working in a hierarchical environment is unimaginable to me. The *ekosistem's* self-conception entails that whoever leaves ruangrupa or *Gudskul* can come back whenever they want.

TCE What is *Gudskul*?

FR A public learning space that we developed with the collectives Serrum and Grafis Huru Hara and cofounded in early 2018. It's the latest articulation of what we think we can be. A school, not as a formal educational institution, but as a place of knowledge production. A space for dissemination and a school of thought.

TCE What you all have in common is the desire to hang out, listen to music, talk, eat together, and be together in a space, in short, immediate contact.

FR Yes, that's right. Cooking, eating, and drinking is what connects us all, as in many other cultures. The pandemic interrupted the possibility of eating together. Normally we eat straight from the table, sharing food without using plates. It tastes better together.

THE SUDDEN RELEASE OF TENSION WAS LIKE STEAM ESCAPING FROM A HIGH-PRESSURE BOILER. NOT ONLY IN THE FIELD OF ART, BUT ALSO IN OTHER AREAS, COLLECTIVES OF VARIOUS KINDS MUSHROOMED.

WE BECAME RUANGRUPA AND MANY OTHER COLLECTIVES FORMED ALONGSIDE US BECAUSE WE ALL REALIZED THAT WE ARE STRONGER UNITED AND CAN ACHIEVE MORE AS A GROUP THAN AS ISOLATED INDIVIDUALS.

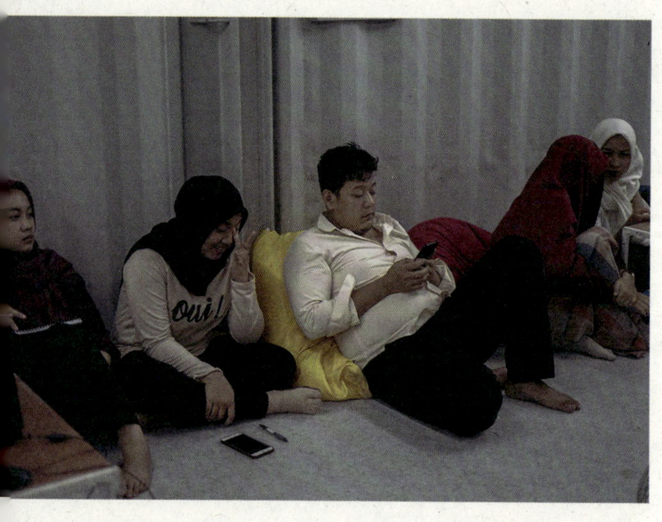
oui

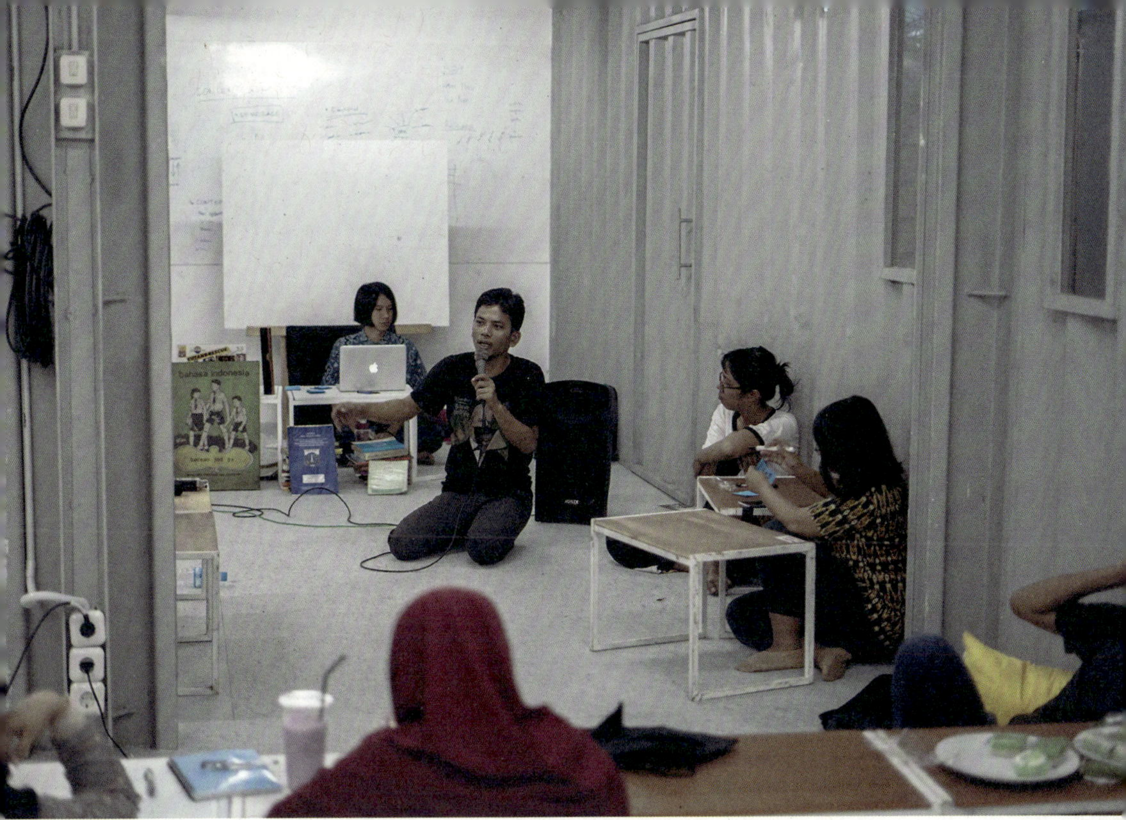

Workshop at *Gudskul*, Jakarta

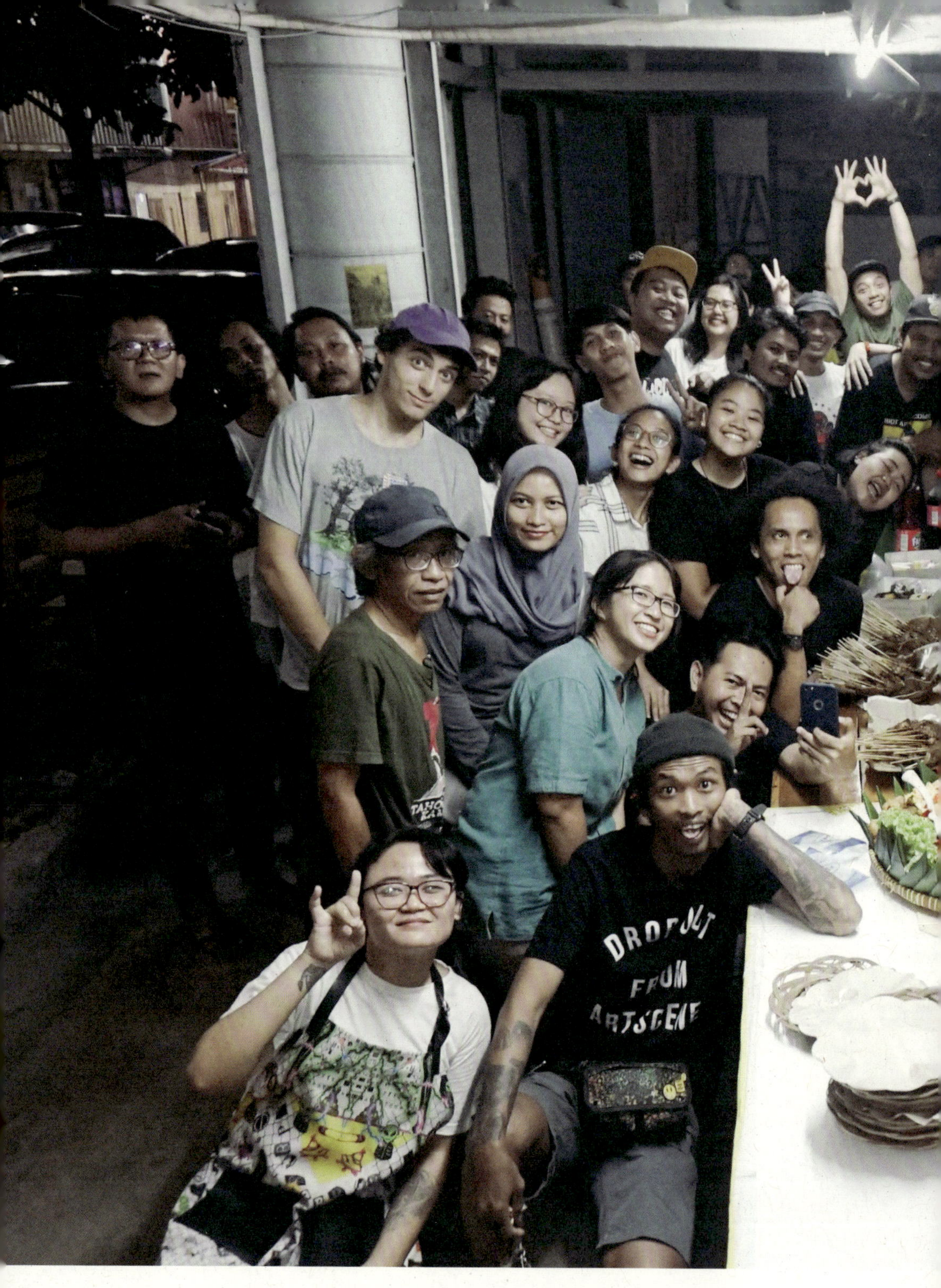
DROPOUT
FROM
ARTSCENE

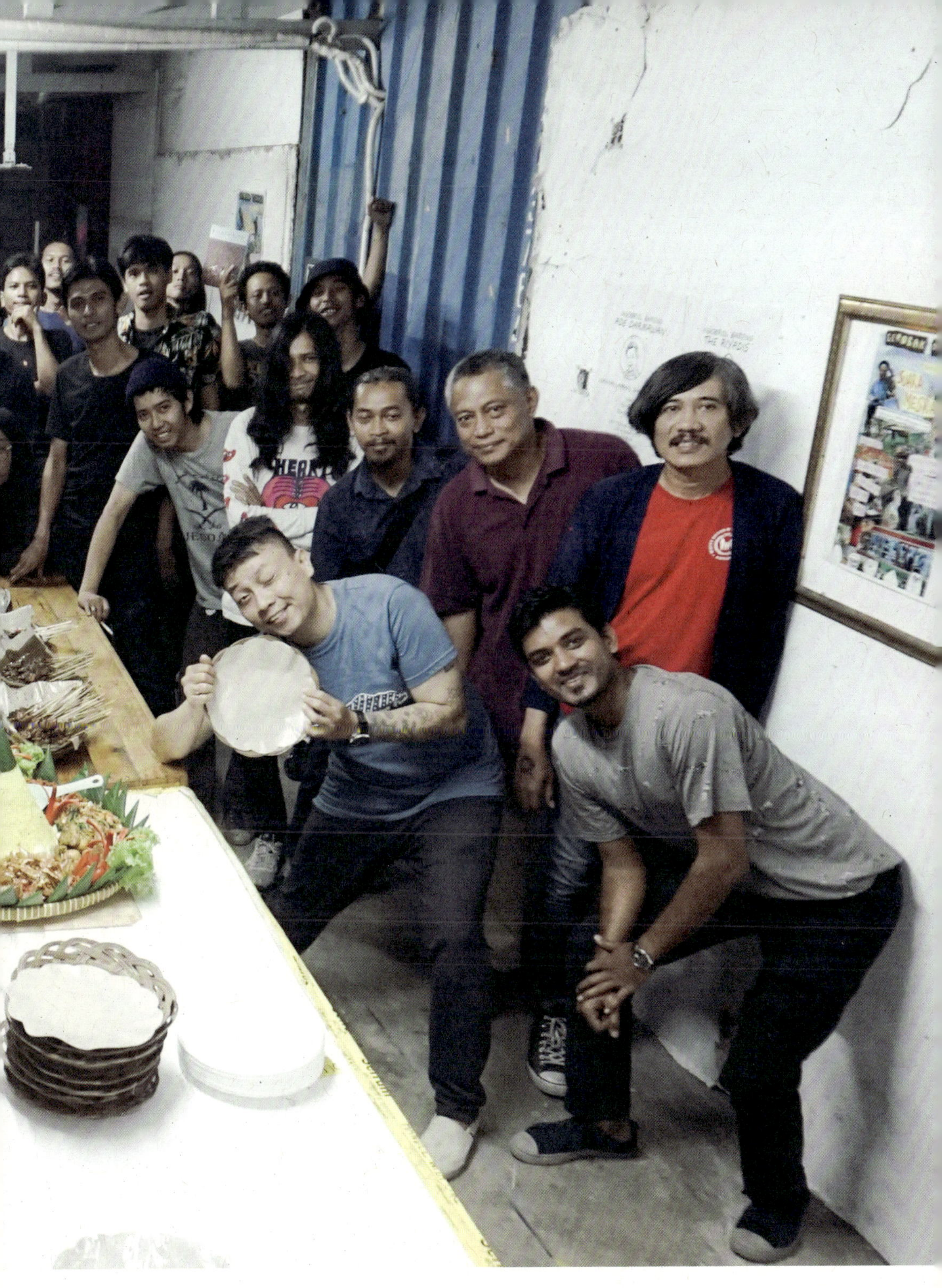

In 2018, the collectives ruangrupa, Serrum and Grafis Huru Hara jointly founded *Gudskul*.

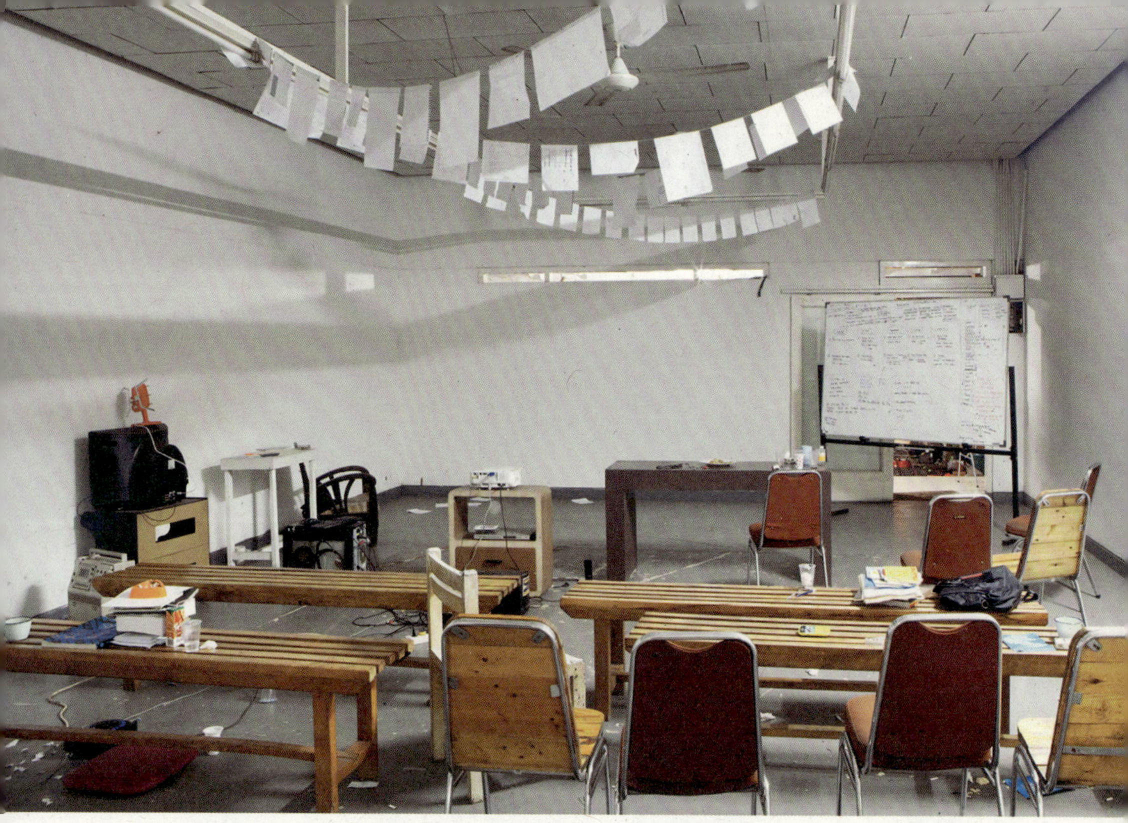

ruangrupas's art is a workshop based work on an ever growing *ekosistem.*

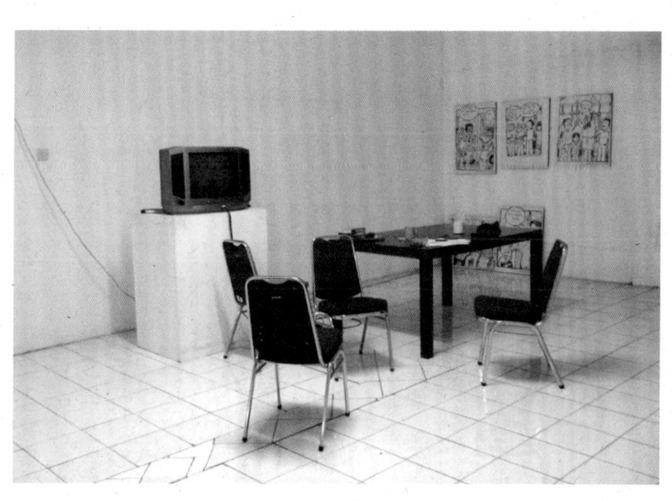

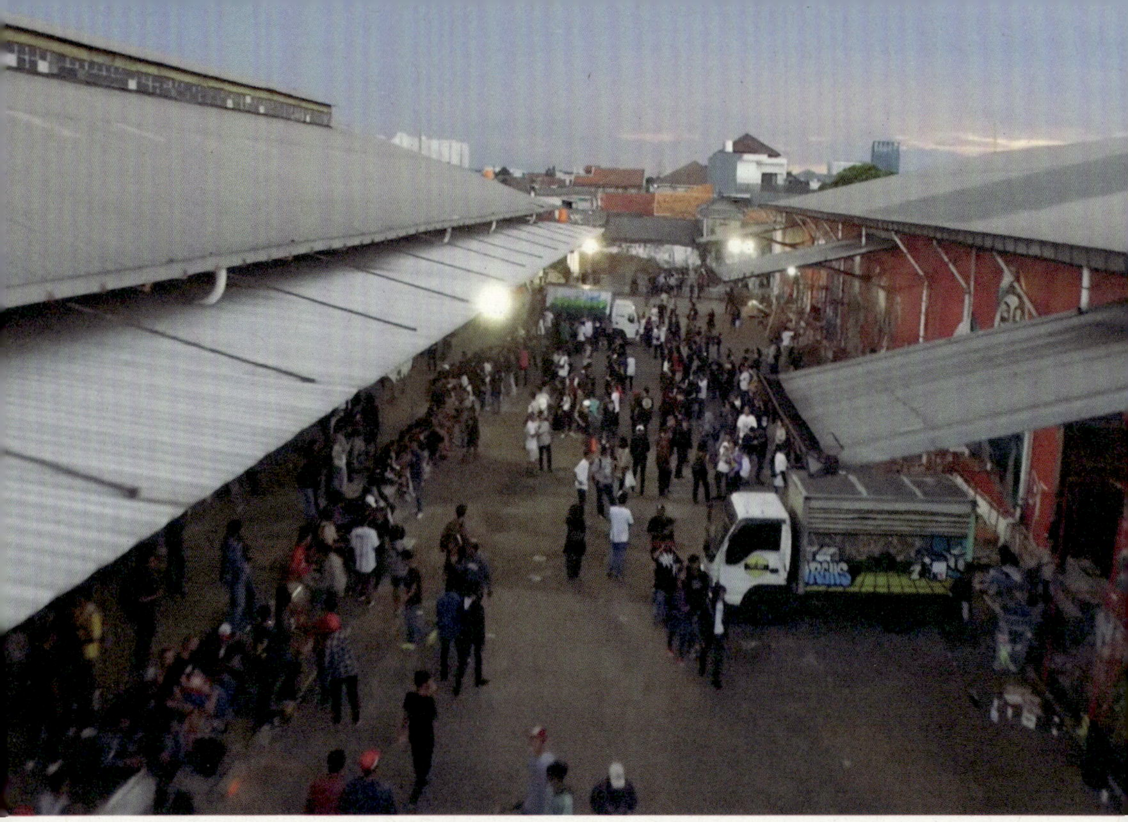

The once closed Gudang Sarinah warehouse complex in Jakarta has been reopened in 2015: a lively venue for exhibitions, bazaars, festivals and music performances. The cross-disciplinary space aims to maintain, cultivate, and establish an integrated support system for creative talents, communities, and various institutions.

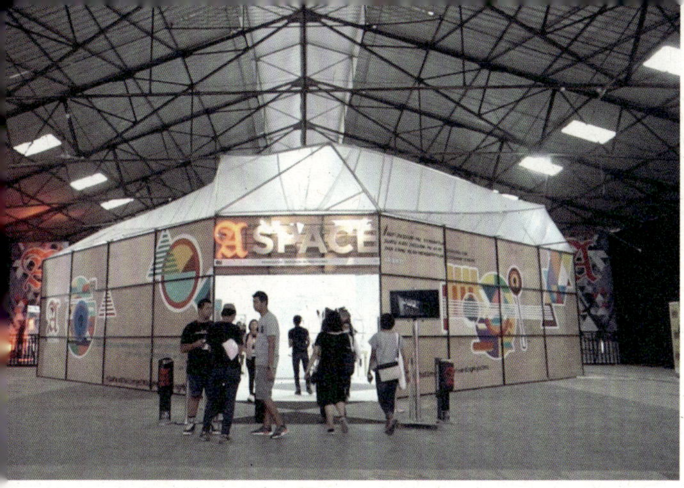

Involved collectives of the *Gundang Sarinah Ekosistem* include ruangrupa itself, for example, with the *RURU Gallery* or *RURUradio.*

ON SPARKS OF INSPIRATION

IN CONVERSATION WITH REZA AFISINA

TCE What happened after the documenta jury's decision?

RA In February 2019, documenta had made the internal decision to entrust us with the artistic direction of the next edition. They told us that the commitment was unofficial and wouldn't be announced until June 2020. We were supposed to keep quiet until then. We used the transitional period to consider the best way to proceed and which of the nine of us would be able to travel and like to live on site. Apart from that, we also worked out the theme together with colleagues from the artistic team. At the very beginning, I told Iswanto, who's always been a very close friend, that it would be better for me to work in Kassel than to constantly fly back and forth. Usually, Indonesians only get a ninety-day visa, and such short stays aren't enough to test the local waters, so to speak.

The situation was similar in Arnhem, where we did the exhibition *SONSBEEK '16: transACTION*, not only inside the museum but also outside in the city. Compared to documenta, *SONSBEEK* was much less intense. On one hand, because I only received a three-month visa and had to leave while it was still running. On the other hand, we couldn't stay longer for financial reasons. That meant we couldn't immerse ourselves in the city and become part of it as deeply as we can in Kassel now. As in Jakarta, it was important to us to mix with the neighbors in Kassel, because we want to find out who the people there are, what kind of work they do, what their hobbies are, which star signs they have. We want to become neighbors ourselves. That takes time, maybe a year, but definitely more than three months. Belonging to the neighborhood also has the advantage of helping you learn more about the environment and its history through the neighbors, because they've lived there for so many years and are familiar with everything. And conversely, I also become a neighbor to others by taking my children to school there, picking them up, going to parent meetings, and getting asked where we come from, who we are, and what we do. This way, the citizens of Kassel who've never been to Indonesia learn about the country I'm from. It has become a daily narrative. Anyone can approach us on the street or at the bakery. That's what a neighborhood is.

We enjoyed staying in Arnhem. It was a nice time but far too short, and it was wonderful to connect with other friends there. It linked up with what we were doing in Jakarta as part of the platform *Gudang Sarinah Ekosistem*, which has existed since 2015, and its development was, after all, about formulating how we can make a structure that enables us to work as a collective with other collectives in cities beyond Jakarta.

By the way, in Arnhem we had a venue similar to the one in Kassel, only it was called *ruru huis* not *ruruHaus*, which in Kassel can be seen directly from the Fridericianum and is located in the former "Sportarena" department store. In Arnhem, it was run by reinaart vanhoe in a former photo studio. He was there a lot; we rarely. In short, for the seven of us in Arnhem, working there was neither effective nor efficient, and also terribly exhausting due to the hassle of obtaining visas for the participating collectives.

Our work on documenta fifteen began with time-consuming research into its history. Of course, we knew about documenta's international significance. But we never pushed our luck, never planned to travel to Kassel. If only because we were deeply involved in our own context and projects; that was something existential for us. Also, there weren't any points of contact between the Indonesian art world, which was completely ignored by the West, and documenta. The latter had neither an open eye nor a sense of Indonesia's contemporary art. Nor did it know anything about the art scene. So dealing with documenta didn't make much sense to us at first. It wouldn't have brought us much either. Moreover, we wouldn't have had the faintest idea about how to approach it. That only changed when we were invited to a biennial. Then it clicked: "Okay, this is it."

Even up to the day we were shortlisted as a curatorial team, we didn't know anything about documenta's history. Nor were we familiar with Kassel as a city. To work here, you have to know it inside out and have experienced it in everyday life. What is Kassel? That was one of the essential starting questions for us.

TCE Was it clear to you from the start that you wanted to come here with the whole family?

RA Yes, because when we calculated everything, it turned out to be very effective and more efficient. Also, it allowed more shared experience. And I'm not the only one glad we took that step; we all are. The ball got rolling with the initiation of the *ruruHaus*, which we completed in July 2020 with the students of the Kunsthochschule Kassel. By now, more than forty individuals or community groups from Kassel are involved in the programming of *ruruHaus*. Over the 100 days, we will supplement some things here and there. They'll be more networked and have accompanying programs to make documenta a good harvest.

Yes, it was wonderful for the children. We arrived in July; it was summer. Compared to the tense situation in Indonesia, where the lockdown hit people much harder than in Germany, everything here felt very fresh and light. You could go to bars and move around freely, whereas in Indonesia you were only allowed to leave the house to go shopping. Also, the walking distances in Kassel are short, public transportation is convenient, everything is easily accessible, which is why the children feel very happy and comfortable here. I can even imagine living here after the documenta. By the way, I've already been to Germany once before thanks to a residency in Hildesheim in 2009. It's the first time for my wife and children.

TCE How did you become a member of ruangrupa?

RA Firstly, ruangrupa doesn't have "members." Secondly, I'm not a founder. I had friendly relations with many people in the group since college days, including Ade. He mainly lived in Jakarta, but studied in Yogyakarta. He traveled back and forth most of the time until 1998, when he went to the Rijksakademie in Amsterdam for two years. During our time at the Jakarta Art Institute, Indra, Daniella, and I hung out constantly, and we also met Ade regularly. After Suharto stepped down in 1998, we felt the need to create something together, which was a need many people of our generation shared at the time. To do this, we needed a space–not a studio space, but rather a place where we could contribute, distribute, or bring something to life together. During that time, the initiative and idea for a space called ruangrupa came from Ade, who was also in the circle of other friends from the art school, and it was realized in 2000. As for how Indra, Daniella, and I participated, in the beginning we were involved in different programs or program formats until we decided to focus on learning and training. So we contributed to things that were directly connected to ruangrupa, but more in the background. Then in 2003, I got a basic salary for the first time. From that moment on, I became more intensely involved with ruangrupa as an organization or collective.

TCE Why did you want to get more involved?

RA Because I admired how they worked individually and because we were friends. I'm from West Java, so not from Jakarta, and I was a student in the cinematography department. The first time I met ruangrupa was as a fan. We hung out together, goofed around, played music gigs.

Under the New Order regime, it was necessary to devise strategies for how we could do this and that and deal with the various connections to the art school in Jakarta or even in other parts of the city. That's where it was an advantage to know Ade, who had connections. Before that, I had worked in other fields, including a large company, but kept returning to ruangrupa, especially between 1999 and 2002. I was in the process of becoming a professional artist but realized I wasn't ready yet and needed to learn more. I was anything but productive from 1997 to 1998, under the political conditions of the regime, especially during the turbulent currency crisis. There was so much I didn't understand, and I was really frustrated. The way the people of ruangrupa dealt with the immense adversities of everyday life felt inspiring and enriching to me; it was a ray of hope, an unforgettable experience. I forged more new relationships than I lost, and they were much closer than the ones with family. The good thing was that we could argue with each other and shared a lot. It wasn't important whether you belonged or not. That's why there isn't any membership. That's how I experienced ruangrupa.

Indra and Daniella were around me since I started out as a student. Nothing has changed between us since then. The basis of everything has stayed the same. We still talk about laziness, and it's still very chill. And if you compare what it was like during our student days back then, when we didn't even exist as a collective, with the situation now at the time of documenta, there isn't any major difference. Only the task is different. Our struggle is always about space, and that's another reason that brought me to ruangrupa. When I was new to Jakarta, I was looking for a home. Sure, you can live there on your own, but that's completely different from feeling at home. When ruangrupa moved into its first house, I used to go there and stay overnight. I met artists from the Rijksakademie who also lived there. In our conversations, I learned a lot about networking and how media art works. With ruangrupa, that rarely happened in the form of presentations; it came up spontaneously during talks. "Okay," we said, "let's have an exchange. This artist from the Netherlands has this or that background, and if you want to meet them and know more, let's meet them." That's how it always was. It had something of a gentle embrace.

TCE It seems it wasn't just you, but everyone in the group who longed for a shared home. Do you think it's a result of the extreme destabilization and uncertainty during the dictatorship?

RA I mean, most of us grew up under the New Order regime, which means that we'd been brainwashed for thirty-two years, and differently than the generations after us. In any case, we found out during that time that we had a shared place where we could do different kinds of experiments. Hungry for knowledge, our conversations revolved around art, around what an artist residency is, what an art project is, what an art lab is, what a publishing house is. That's what we talked about. Not knowing what an artist collective was, we didn't call ourselves one, but rather a space initiated by artists. We didn't just want to make an appearance as individuals, but primarily as a group of artists who lived and worked together. At the time, it seemed like everyone was questioning the idea of collectivity.

TCE How did you personally experience the political situation as a student?

RA It was the era of Suharto's rule, but also a golden age of music. I think most Southeast Asian countries like Singapore, Indonesia, Malaysia, the Philippines, and Brunei Darussalam were quite similar. They had comparable political ideas to Indonesia, and they had a similar vision of Southeast Asia. When I was still getting my bearings, I was initially unaware that both the art academy and the heart of political power were located right in the center of the city. We didn't care about politics. But in 1997, we started getting worried about how things were going politically. That was the year of the parliamentary elections, and it seemed like that election would have been Suharto's last term. Yet he was re-elected.

I had a punk band that advocated for a new party, the People's Democratic Party. In order not to draw attention from the United States, which always equates leftism with communism, the new party didn't officially present itself as left-wing, even though it was. Then, during the Academy's anniversary in 1997, we performed on large trucks that drove around the city. Because of our support for the party, we feared the military might intervene and disrupt the event. That's why most of the band members went into hiding three months before the elections. At the same time, the situation was extremely tense due to the devastating Asian crisis, which resulted in no one being able to find a decent job or earn any money. So we suddenly understood that we were confronted with these political issues. Of course we already knew about the Indonesian political context because we lived in Jakarta, but somehow we hadn't connected one thing with another. We were still blind to the connections. Some of the major universities had their own parliament that dealt with the student movement. But the art school didn't pay us much attention. Due to the convenient location in the city center, a lot of friends from other universities dropped in on us. So the campus sometimes became a kind of meeting place, and we felt that we had to be prepared for political unrest. On July 27, 1997, the day of the uprising, we were celebrating the campus anniversary with an international dance festival. Clueless of what was actually brewing at the time, we were just looking forward to meeting friends and having fun. Not much came of that. The disputes between the supporters of different political parties escalated and turned into a mass riot; many sought shelter with us. We were naïve enough to believe that the military wouldn't enter the campus, but the military is the military. They swept us away and destroyed everything. Somebody yelled they were entering the campus, and one of my friends said, "Hey, we have marines here!" Indeed, circumstance would have it that the band of the marines had been invited, some of whose members were our friends. Due to their presence, the army assumed we were under Marine surveillance. They held us for 24 hours because they thought the rebels were there.

TCE Did this experience of having your space violated make you realize how important it is to have your own?

RA It might be that we also have a special relationship with having a space where we feel safe as a result of these experiences. The reasons why we cared so much about it are different, namely the ones already mentioned. During my studies, when I was living on campus for a few years because I didn't have any other choice, we were looking for ways to create our own space, not only to make art, but also to question the various teaching methods used in the academy. We wanted to know what a curator does. What a good art library entails. How the art market works. What constitutes the global context. We needed that space to develop our own ideas about the most diverse things, how experiences can become a method of learning. Nothing works by saying, "According to the art school curriculum, I learned it like so and so." Actual knowledge is based on experience and on how we do things, explore things, and also distribute things. The new media that were just emerging and starting to take hold also piqued our curiosity. Jakarta back then didn't have much to do with all of that.

To set up artist residencies, like we did from 2001 to 2007, we had to find out what a residency was in the first place. After all, it isn't just about inviting close friends we like to hang out, drink, eat, and party with, but also about contributing something. They came up to us and said, "Hey, you're working on this topic right now and we want to contribute something to it because we have this background." These are things that we practiced in Jakarta.

HUNGRY FOR KNOWLEDGE, OUR CONVERSATIONS REVOLVED AROUND ART, AROUND WHAT AN ARTIST RESIDENCY IS, WHAT AN ART PROJECT IS, WHAT AN ART LAB IS, WHAT A PUBLISHING HOUSE IS. THAT'S WHAT WE TALKED ABOUT. NOT KNOWING WHAT AN ARTIST COLLECTIVE WAS, WE DIDN'T CALL OURSELVES ONE, BUT RATHER A SPACE INITIATED BY ARTISTS.

DAYDREAMS AND BIG CITY CHAOS

TCE Speaking of Jakarta, how intertwined is ruangrupa with the big city atmosphere?

RA Jakarta is a source of inspiration. We all associate the city with daydreams. It's an accommodating city, even if it doesn't make it easy to live and work there. From the very beginning, we believed that even if it couldn't fulfill our dreams, at least we can share them with others who come from different islands, regions, provinces, cities big and small. I chose Jakarta because I was curious about this huge complex city with its secrets and possibilities, how it deals with the variety and diversity of views of life, how they fit in or make themselves felt in a life so bustling and fast-paced. Some abandon their ideologies as soon as they come to Jakarta. I never experienced this in Bandung, which is quite similar to Bali or even Yogyakarta. Things are a bit more relaxed there. It doesn't have that fast pace. Everyone enjoys their daily necessities. Being highly preoccupied and spending a lot of time in traffic jams, people experience everyday life in Jakarta completely differently. You can take something and learn from everything you see and hear. Most of my friends, Daniella, Indra, Ade, farid, Julia, and Ajeng were born and raised in Jakarta, while Iswanto and I each grew up in a different province then moved to Jakarta. This messy city not only inspired our ways of life, but also helped us establish our artistic abilities with respect to our work that relates to the center of politics and government. Jakarta is also a good place to make various new friends, who either approach you or you end up meeting on the street. It gives you the feeling of sharing a lot of things with each other.

When I rented a room there, Jakarta was flooded, and several hundreds of thousands of people had to leave their homes. Everyone was immediately available and connected with each other–not out of any obligation to help each other, but because the situation required it. You know, helping people is a way of showing off, in a good sense: we do it as part of the community and because you are important to our neighborhood. Even if I don't know you, you still live here, right? So Jakarta generates so-called personal landmarks, which is nice. By regularly sitting or being somewhere, you become a landmark for others. For us, it's really romantic and fulfilling. I mean, Jakarta is tough, very tough actually. If you're modest, this city is enough. It's part of our engine.

TCE What else makes Jakarta so diverse?

RA I come from a wealthy family that was suddenly impoverished, and because we were penniless we couldn't visit other cities or islands anymore. Made up of 17,000 islands, Indonesia is rich in culture and beliefs, not just religious ones. What I found most fulfilling is the culture of cooking and drinking. If you want to experience this diversity in all its richness, you're better off in a big city like Jakarta. It gives you endless opportunities to learn from others. That's something I never really had where I grew up. Sure, I had many friends there, but living there didn't really present any challenges. Jakarta just forces you to live differently. Even when working together, we shared a lot of things, but our survival strategies differed. For example, I worked as a street magician, while some of my friends who were performance artists from the theater faculty earned their money with short performances in busses. I mainly worked as a sound engineer on documentaries. But then the economic crisis came, everything collapsed, and I had nothing left but a bag of clothes. When I was completely hopeless, my friends told me "You can stay on campus, there's a studio, water, and electricity." That's what I did until I met ruangrupa. When I asked if they had a room for me, they welcomed me. They also showed the same hospitality to my other friends. They felt that even though Jakarta wasn't fulfilling our dreams yet, we were already living those dreams by being connected and working in the same space. It was hard to find the same kind of working and living conditions that ruangrupa offered. We realized how lucky we actually were.

We weren't the only ones to form a group in 2000. There were a lot of different collectives. A lot of them were more professional than us. They had artist residencies and departments for labs. "Wow," we thought, "this is great. This is something for us." But three years later, a lot of the NGOs were suddenly gone. We feared that we'd also have to stop in a few years when the funding ran out. But we've been around for more than twenty years by now.

TCE You don't just work together as a collective, you almost spend your whole lives together.

RA That was important for us until many of us started families. I can't exactly tell you how ruangrupa is embedded in our families or how collectivity is practiced there. I have two children, Iswanto three, Andan one. Indra, Ajeng, Ade, Iswanto, and Sari are married, and Daniella is a single mother of three. Ruangrupa thus became rhizomatic, meaning interlinked with diverse forms of family. For example, when ruangrupa was in financial trouble and poor, of course our families were affected. But we were still able to live the spirit of ruangrupa. It was really astonishing, and we never thought we would give up ruangrupa and find a real job. Even in those damn hard times, we were able to share things with each other. That wasn't only the case with us, but also with other collectives like Serrum and Grafis Huru Hara, which we're in *Gudskul* with. They had similar practices, but in their own context. We learned the legal basics from them, which we were able to apply over the years in order to give ruangrupa a legal form. It was about the basic requirements necessary to generate sources of income. We thought it was a good and smart idea that we followed up on years later, after ruangrupa decided to establish itself as a small organization. Serrum were the ones who formulated it, and we were the ones who considered different strategies, made suggestions, and contacted networks with different financial models. Those who worked mainly in the studio base presented their practices, and we were provided with different tools. It was a balancing act between our needs and our business group, which dealt with collective goods and could sell our proposals. That's what made it possible for us to fully focus on the artistic practices. Before, Ade, Indra, and I used to deal with proposals. Now it was the business group that dealt with it. They would ask us for the artistic concepts for the funders or possible supporting partners, so they could understand what we were doing and what we wanted. That's the way we've worked so far, and it's the model we use in Jakarta.

TCE Crossovers are a given for ruangrupa, insofar as you don't have any hierarchies between media; you don't privilege literature, film, music, or dance. How do you share experiences and knowledge of the different media?

RA Our conversations run in a lot of different directions, and not just because we're interested in a lot of things. So sometimes our meetings are not so straightforward, effective, or efficient. When it comes to decisions, it's sometimes hard to explain why a decision wasn't made. It was actually up for discussion, but we ended up talking about completely different things.

THE DIVERSITY OF INDIVIDUAL INTERESTS IN THE COLLECTIVE

TCE You're all interested in very different forms of artistic expression.

RA Yes, while Andan has a passion for movies and books, speaks Arabic, French, and German, many were interested in music, for example, and another in management. Iswanto loves jazz, but of all people, the person who didn't like jazz made the case for doing a jazz festival. We realized how we could connect with each other in a very natural way, without having any concrete formulations of our goal at hand. In this context, I have to think of our *Siasat* guide. The word siyasah comes from Arabic, and in Indonesian it means both investigation and criticism, but also politics, cunning, tactics, and reasoning used to achieve certain goals. In this guide, we included several pieces that we call fruitnotes. To put it differently: we've done exhibitions, worked as project managers, and have been able to see things grow. So it makes sense to harvest the "fruits." They became a kind of guideline we could use to see what our practice is based on and which developments it can embrace. It's been ten years since we made this guide. And if I'm not mistaken, we tried to put it into practice in 2011 at the Asian Triennial in Manchester, and that was the first time we started questioning it. The fact that *Siasat* wasn't fully elaborated. We were tired and exhausted, both from the New Order regime's brainwashing and the politics of education in Asia. The education system focused on traditional educational paths and learning methods–exclusively bilateral, but never multilateral connections. Doing it on our terms meant developing our own articulations. Each person in this world would probably first start speaking from the perspective of their own local conditions. We partly drew on Western terms to help us articulate ourselves. Years ago, when we realized we needed artist initiatives, we asked ourselves if we should call ourselves one. While we were studying, we had no idea what that even was. But Ade knew the term from Amsterdam and brought that ingredient to Jakarta. Once we took a look at Airbnb's business model and thought that when an artist rents an apartment to work there, it becomes a kind of artist residency, but with the small difference that the Airbnb's landlord makes money from it and the artist doesn't. Strange! So we have to learn how to articulate ourselves in our context. I mean, the things we've learned or followed and the concepts that shaped us often come from the Western context. But we also need something that can supplement that particular context. Things that supposedly come from the Western world have actually proven to be quite practical for us. They reinforce other things that are happening in Indonesia.

How can we pass on what we've experienced and practice to others? After all, it isn't taught at our art colleges. Academic training is usually quite different. At one university you get taught this, at another you learn something else. But neither discusses what an artist residency is, for example.

In the general discourse, there's a lot of talk about what a public space or a space for the public is. We're trying to make more sense of it. How about we still work together in these foggy conditions and let someone who has directions take us by the hand, someone who knows their way around, or someone who doesn't, and sometimes we just end up getting lost. That's how we practice it in Kassel.

In *ruruHaus*, the boundary between what is related to our so-called official documenta fifteen and its program, and what isn't, is quite fluid. That's because many of our friends in Kassel do not contribute directly to *ruruHaus* or documenta, but want to create something.

To blur that divide, we subsume everything under what we call the "Kassel ekosistem."

TCE You don't seem to give the artistic collaborators and collectives any guidelines.

RA The collectives, artists who are officially invited and legally secured by documenta, work within the official program. Instead of telling them what to do, we just turned on the tap to let the ideas bubble up. This is in line with our spontaneous thinking. If we had proceeded by first trying to connect them to the documenta, a lot of things would have stalled and failed from the very start. Practical experience in Jakarta has taught us that. I don't know whether our way of thinking is compatible with the European-German context, and most of all whether it can disturb the methodologies of a European mindset, philosophically speaking. It remains to be seen whether the documenta can be experienced in a way where people say, to use a different image, the food is good, but too salty for me, and the cake delicious, but too sweet for me. The ideal documenta fifteen would be disruptive but good.

By the way, I've been wondering how we suddenly ended up getting involved in this particular task out of nowhere, that is, coming from far away and continuing the *Gudskul ekosistem* in Kassel. Arriving with this baggage, we worked from the very beginning on the premise that everyone shares their resources. We wouldn't have agreed without documenta's willingness to do this. The good thing is that the institutions, all these families and partners got directly involved. Yes, it's a nice experience that documenta allows so many options despite its rather rigid construction. I see an analogy here to German football, which taught me a lot. From an Indonesian point of view, it's rigid in terms of its very structured formation, midfield, attack, defense, and each position is very strong.

TCE And sometimes the players don't have any flow. (laughs)

RA There are a lot of things we learn from. A lot of collectives and groups that we've met in Germany are registered as an association, and it has encouraged us to establish similar structures. We do have a legal structure for social clubs and other organized public-interest communities in Indonesia, but hardly anyone would think of doing things on that legal basis. First, because no one supports them. Second, because we wouldn't get good feedback if we built an organization on a legal basis. Third, because it is not profitable for us. If you create a legal structure in Germany, you also gain opportunities in terms of financial support from cultural foundations, but that isn't the case in Indonesia.

THE TOTAL TRANSFORMATION OF KASSEL

TCE Do you have the impression that the “Kassel ekosistem” is starting to work? Can you feel where it’s going?

RA A lot of things were already working and inspiring for us when we first came to Kassel in 2019 and met some of the collectives. There were already a lot of different potentials here, even in so-called rural Kassel, which includes the growing street culture, community and youth center. During the yearly presentations, we also got to know an outstanding collective from the art school here. We also visited the gallery festival, which was being held here for the first time. That was before the pandemic.

TCE When documenta opens its doors every five years, Kassel undergoes a total transformation. But no sooner are the 100 days over than everything falls back into its normal state. The documenta is something like a bubble that bursts after its end. Your curatorial intention is more about sustainability in relation to the city and its actors. Did you exchange ideas about this phenomenon with local collectives and groups before and after documenta?

RA Yes, our initial question was: what happens before, during, and after documenta? Up close, we only know the before so far. As part of our *ekosistem*, documenta fifteen is one of the gardens in which various types of flowers or fruits are already growing sporadically. Actually, anyone going to documenta is also interwoven with Kassel. Therefore, we were asking ourselves why the people who have the great fortune of experiencing this major exhibition only talk about the shows, but not about Kassel. After all, those who come to Jakarta also want to know what the reality is like, what its peculiarities, advantages, and disadvantages are. Why the traffic is so dramatic. Compared to Bangkok it isn't so bad, compared to Manila still bearable, and for us quite annoying. Being stuck in a traffic jam for six hours, not in a car but on a motorcycle, is borderline.

Our wish is that other friends experience a city like Kassel in this sense. Now many collectives are coming together, creating their own ways to finance themselves in the process, and eventually joining ruangrupa in a common practice. And we ask ourselves: how do we see their practices? How do they relate to ours? Are there collectives among them with a way of working that is somewhat comparable to ours? Can we invite them to our platform that functions as a place of exchange?

The documenta fifteen, as we are designing it, is of course different from previous editions. As I've read and heard, Okwui Enwezor and Adam Szymczyk both tried to incorporate what we call the "Kassel ekosistem" into this celebration. And that is a big challenge for us as well.

By the way, we also used the idea of the *ekosistem* for the Jakarta Biennale, where Ade and farid collaborated. There, the *ekosistem* was also the source they drew from. Underlying the projects in Jakarta was the question of how to create inclusive access for residents in the context of a city with these immense dimensions. This was considerably more difficult to accomplish than in Kassel, where we met the students of the art academy right at the start. They're involved with everything happening in the city and share their experiences with us. With the biennial in Jakarta, the process was completely different. People come to work with us, and as soon as they realize that it doesn't meet their expectations, they leave. In terms of structure, everything is open. We don't have any barriers. The doors are never closed.

TCE Can you describe your method? How does the collaboration with artists and collectives work?

RA We don't delegate or assign anything, but exchange and share in the spirit of our *lumbung* practice. Although, when we started working on documenta fifteen, the pandemic wasn't looming ahead yet. So we weren't forced to only work digitally, but we were still looking for a more effective way to collaborate instead of having nine of us travel to scout out the program. Not only did it seem inefficient, it didn't really suit us. We sent out emails that opened with the question: "What are you working on right now?" Then the Covid pandemic suddenly broke out, and we were forced to do almost everything digitally.

One reason we chose the *lumbung* practice for documenta is that in terms of the collectives, we found some similarities in their energies and spirits. The other is that *lumbung* is a model for sustainable collaboration, so that what emerges can continue to grow after documenta fifteen. Furthermore, we already had working relationships and friendships with artist collectives such as the RAIN (Rijksakademie Artist Initiative International Network) collective, which Ade founded in 2000.

We're finding out how useful it is to build a bridge between us. If my resource is useful to you and yours is useful to me, I make sure I can trust and rely on you to open up your resource to other friends. If you don't have sugar, you ask your neighbor for it. When I was very young and living with my mother, I would go out every day to ask for a bowl of rice because we didn't have any. We were very poor. We also didn't have a toilet, so we had to use the community toilet and clean it. For us, this was natural.

THE GLOBAL CULTURE OF SHARING

TCE You've been used to sharing since childhood. Do other collectives have difficulties with this culture?

RA It probably seems difficult because of the different ways of working. But it isn't a problem to relate to other practices that we aren't familiar with. You can find what we call *lumbung* in all cultures. There are different models of sharing, like cooperation for example. When farmers share a well for their flocks of sheep and meet there to talk, they are creating a shared space. All in all, *lumbung* has a very loose meaning in our conception. I would put it this way: if you see *lumbung* as a symbolic structure, there is nothing wrong with that. If it has a different function in our context than in yours, we will explain it.

TCE *lumbung* is a metaphor for you.

RA Yes, we call it software.

TCE What does *lumbung* mean?

RA When it is harvest time in Indonesia, the surplus isn't used up, but collected and stored in the *lumbung*. It becomes something the community can draw on in times of scarcity, such as a climate disaster or famine. By storing the surplus of resources, farmers give themselves time to rest and the soil a chance to recover. We see *lumbung* as a principle for cooperation, based on generosity and empathy. Sustainability is only guaranteed when resources are continuously renewed and replenished.

JAKARTA IS A SOURCE OF INSPIRATION. WE ALL ASSOCIATE THE CITY WITH DAYDREAMS. IT'S AN ACCOMMODATING CITY, EVEN IF IT DOESN'T MAKE IT EASY TO LIVE AND WORK THERE.

THINGS THAT SUPPOSEDLY COME FROM THE WESTERN WORLD HAVE ACTUALLY PROVEN TO BE QUITE PRACTICAL FOR US. THEY REINFORCE OTHER THINGS THAT ARE HAPPENING IN INDONESIA.

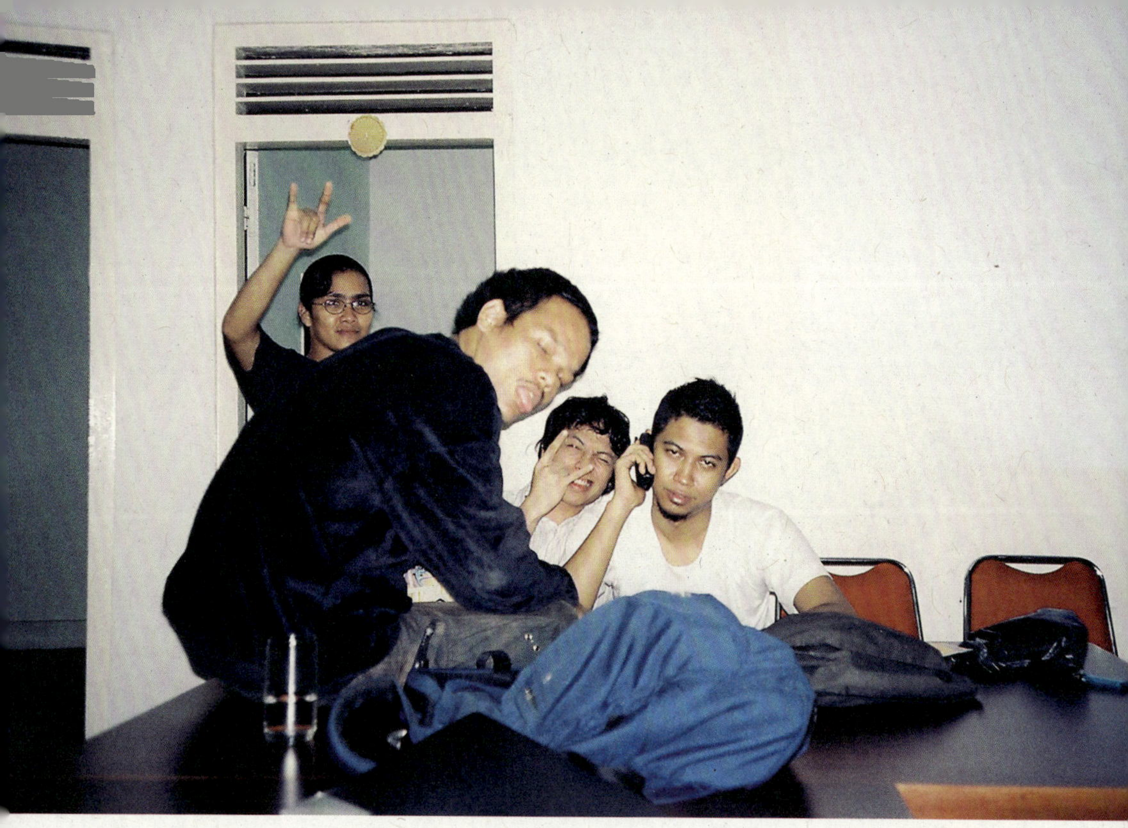

RAIN meeting, 2002

Workshop *SILENT FORCES*, 2001

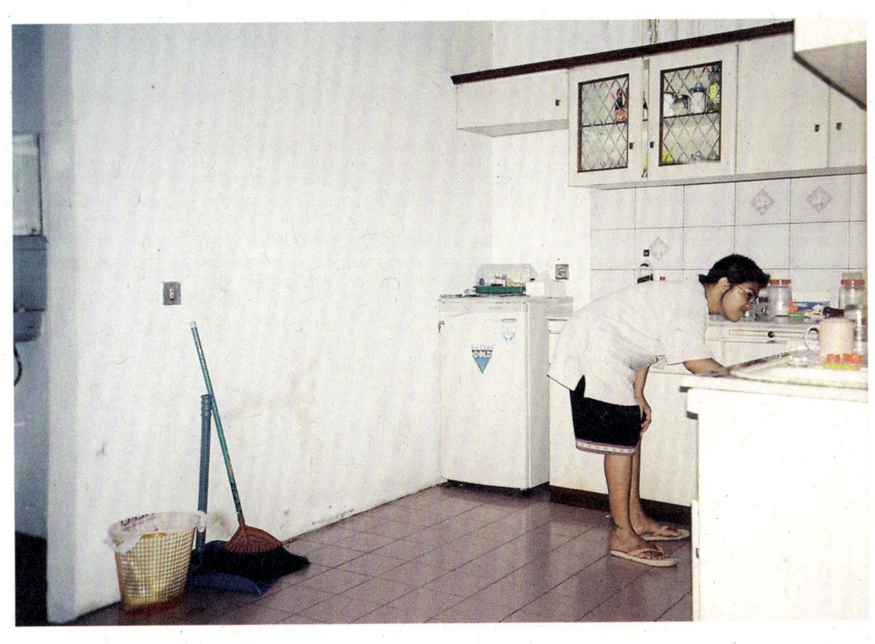

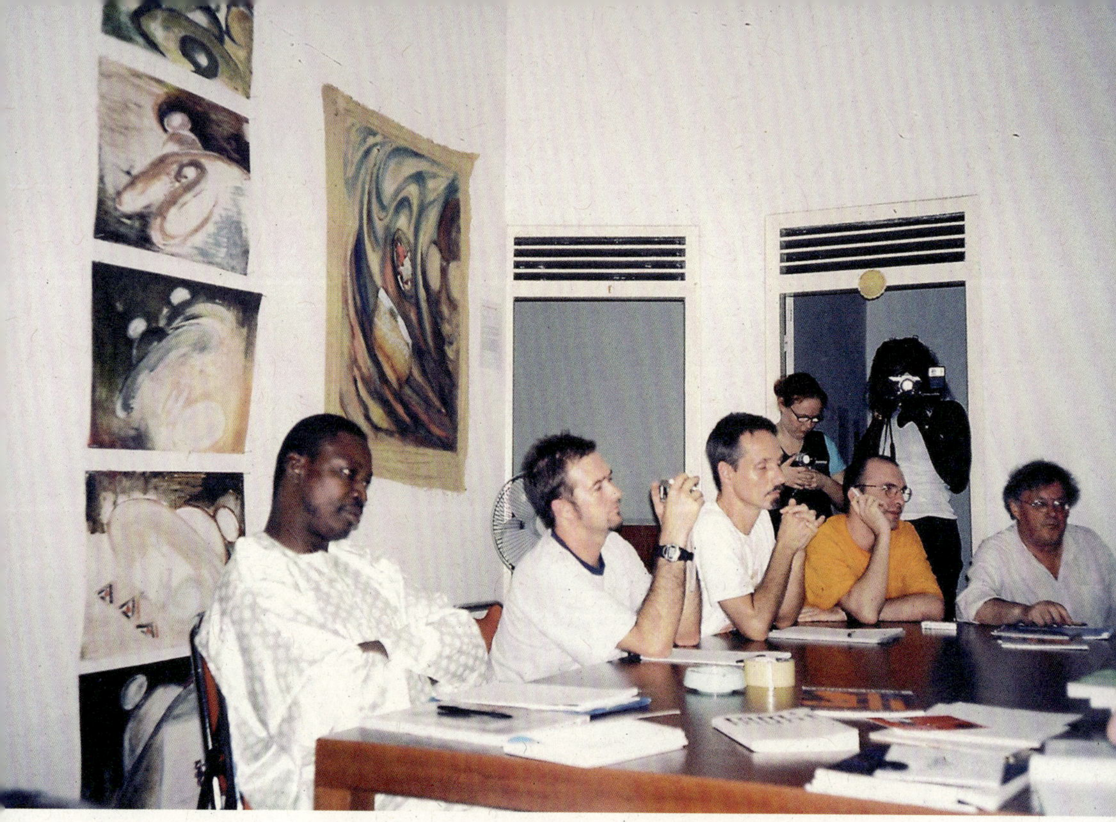

International exchange at the RAIN (Rijksakademie Artist Initiative International Network) meeting, 2002

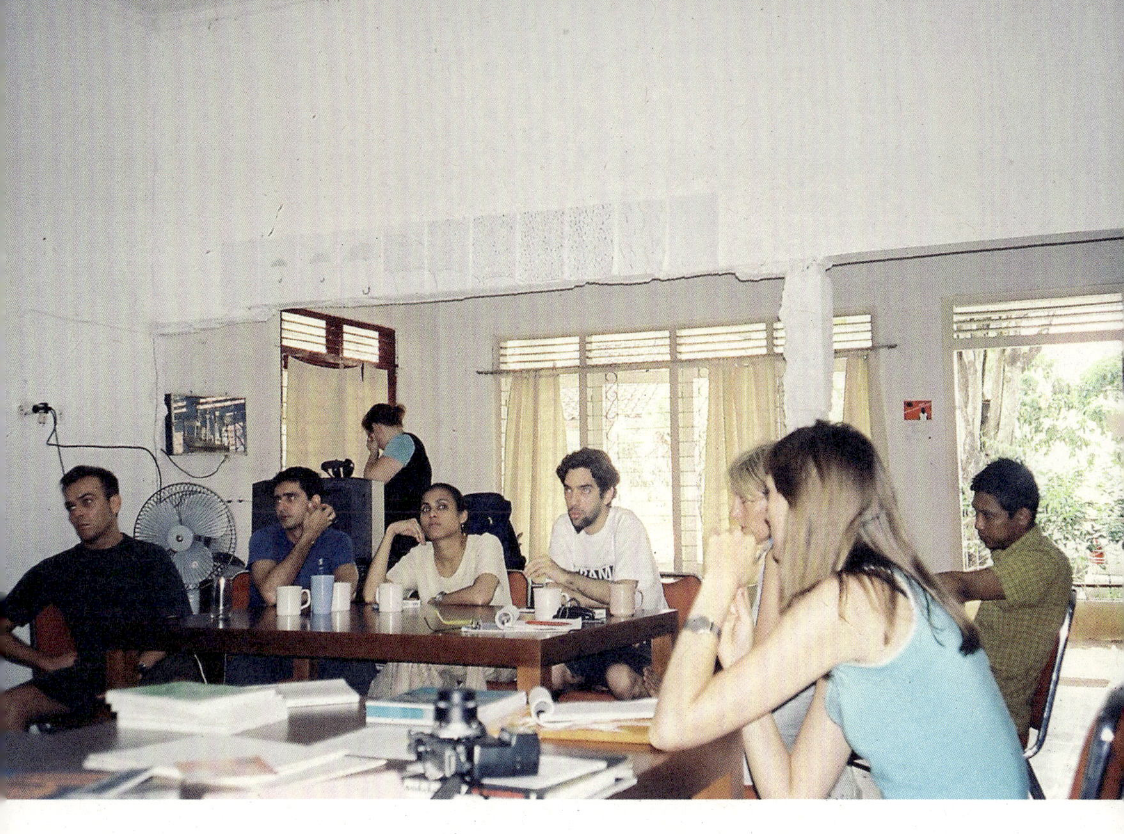

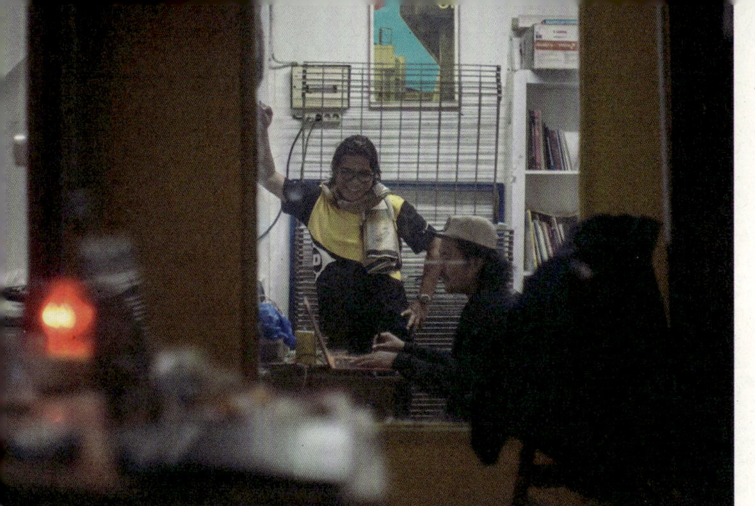

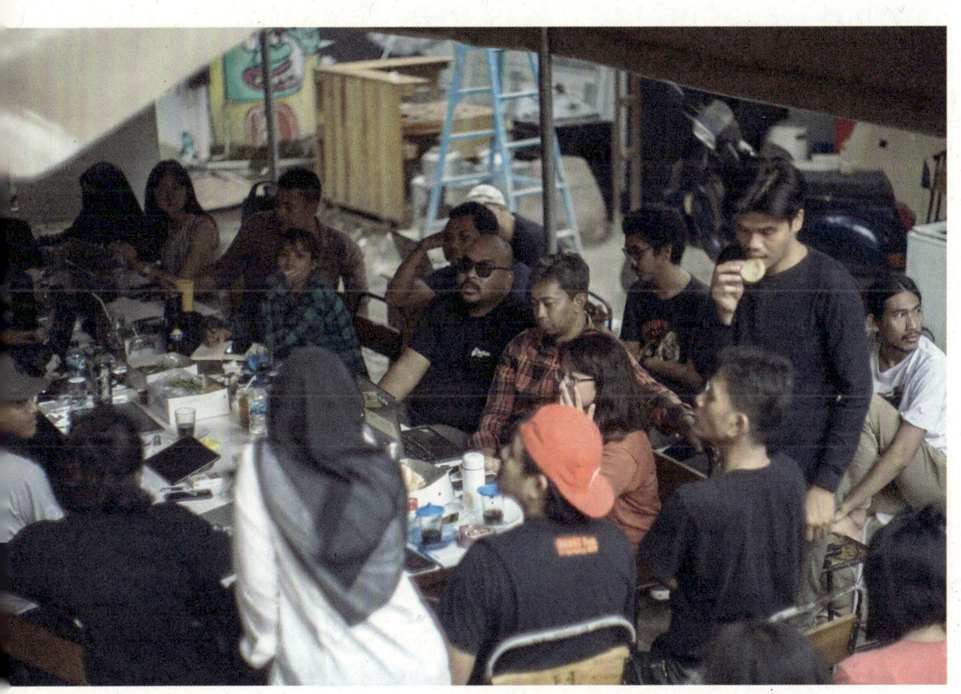

Gudskul is an urban center based on friendship, equality and solidarity in Jakarta

TCE For you, *lumbung* is an artistic and economic model. It stands for sharing resources and caring for each other, as you've said. How did you come to call your curatorial and artistic concept *lumbung*?

RA Yes, it's very interesting. When documenta asked us for a title for the fifteenth edition, we didn't want the title to be some kind of creed. So we were looking for a name from the Indonesian context that would denote our practice of sharing and everything that's happened to us and become part of previous experiences with the *Gudskul ekosistem*. The question was: does a name for these ideals and ways of working already exist in our society? The term cooperation didn't fit because it comes from a foreign language. We thought of "Istiqlal," the name of the big mosque in Jakarta, which means freedom. But it was also not an option. Then we asked ourselves: how do art, activism, the dissemination of knowledge, the practice of sharing, and the so-called circular economic model work in our context? And thus we came across the idea of *lumbung*. The term's roots in agriculture touch on a variety of aspects. If there's enough stock, even those who aren't part of the community can take from it when needed. The reason why we didn't come up with *lumbung* as a name right away, even though it was so obvious, had to do with the fact that the word had slipped our minds. Just like the name of a neighbor doesn't come to mind, even though you know it.

In science, a name is assigned to an unexplored phenomenon, which then becomes the subject of science. Let's take the example of a flower species from another region of the world that arrives in the Western world. There it is the first to be named by biologists, although it already has a name in its country of origin. The renaming is done for reasons of untranslatability, which astonishes a visitor from the country of origin.

In the course of our research, we found that Europe has its own ideas of *lumbung*, and different forms can also be found in the Indonesian context. A tobacco kiosk can become a *lumbung* for customers because they borrow money there, get over-the-counter medicines, or because they meet, either to chat with each other or to exchange ideas because they are worried about their children, have problems with their wife, or can't cope with the death of a loved one and want to talk it out. Even if the kiosk isn't called *lumbung*, there's still this same spirit of sharing. To us, it feels like we're throwing stones into the water with what we're opening up, and they're bouncing back to us.

TCE How do the intercollective communication processes work within the framework of documenta?

RA Almost every day, everyone participates in what we call an assembly, and at the same time the participating collectives hold their own smaller assemblies.

As a rule, we don't suggest anything to the artists. Instead, we knock on the door asking, "Hey, may I come in? It's been so long since we've met. What are you doing right now?" That's how we got the conversation going. While organizing documenta fifteen, it was also important to gather suggestions from our friends and ask for their consent to make the material, catalogs, and other things available to everyone else as a resource. Some didn't have any problem with that, some didn't want to, while others felt dissatisfied with their own proposals and introduced us to other friends or networks whom they felt would be more appropriate instead. The decisive factor was the agreement to exchange one's own resources with others. Some collectives just told us what they'd like to do, but not much more.

TCE Can you pick a few contributions as examples?

RA There are some collectives that participate in other collective activities. For example, the members of Arts

Collaboratory, who are collaborating with collectives that will organize different platforms during the 100 days, or Cinema Caravan, who either share their objects and structures with other collectives or with part of the "Kassel ekosistem." There are individual artists like reinaart vanhoe, who has developed ideas about how he envisions collaborating with collectives. Agus Nur Amal PMTOH, an artist from Aceh (Sumatra), usually works with artists, photographers, videographers, educators, and in the context of documenta fifteen, students in Kassel. He chose his starting points–Jacob and Wilhelm Grimm's fairy tales, the cultivation of oral tradition, and the processing of trauma–against the backdrop of his investigation into post-traumatic stress after the tsunami event in 2004, where many of his friends lost their lives.

We aren't the ones who assign artists a place to work–rather, they chose them on their own. The Jatiwangi art Factory–an artist collective of more than fifty multimedia artists, musicians, designers, and curators working in a former clay tile factory in Jatisura, Indonesia–cooperate with a factory for roofing tiles in Kassel. They engage with the conditions of their environment and postcolonial history of the space. At the time of their arrival, we were considering the Hübner site as a venue since it was vacant, but hadn't decided on it yet. When the Jatiwangi art Factory learned about the existence of the former industrial area in the east of Kassel, they wanted to visit the site immediately, and since they were kindly welcomed there, they chose the location for themselves.

Many artists have a strong relationship to space, and sometimes several artists or collectives had set their sights on the same place. They would discuss their relationships to the place with each other and why it was so important to them. Often enough they agreed on sharing the place.

THE BRIDGE BETWEEN CENTER AND PERIPHERY

TCE By not only working with documenta's legendary sites, but also the industrial area, you're building a bridge between the center and the periphery. You're also integrating the premises of the boat rental company Ahoi in Unterneustadt on the banks of the Fulda.

RA Yes, our approach revolves around the river. It's a part of our body, along with the documenta. We live in Jakarta near the Ciliwung and love the river flowing past. Since Kassel lives with the Fulda, we thought why not activate the river. And fortunately, the people from the Ahoy property responded to our proposal for doing something there with the utmost enthusiasm and collaboration.

So did Hafenstraße 76, which is connected to the waterfront. Doing something there had been part of our plan from the beginning, but not in such a way that we wanted to make the east the focus; but it turned out that there was a lot going on there and many artists discovered something relevant to their projects. For example, the Platz der Deutschen Einheit located in the eastern part of Kassel, which is a symbol of unification and a point of connection to the eastern part of the city. It's exciting to see how some of the artists drew on the idea of psychogeography and engaged with the particular history of the city's eastern side, on the "other" side of the river, so to speak. What happens in the transitions between the different parts of the city? First, we got a sense of walking distances and public transportation connections, then inquired if there were neighborhood associations.

The choice of venues developed quite organically, as you can see, step by step. We told most of our friends that they should work with their own space. Many of them who had one available invited us to visit. Some spaces could be connected to documenta, others couldn't. It had to be coordinated with the capacities of the production and infrastructure team. One example: when we first visited Hafenstraße 76, we were skeptical when we saw the building, even though it had once functioned as a food storage building. It seemed like it would need a lot of adjustments. We gave it the name Hafenstraße 76 because of its location. After researching the local conditions–namely how the place relates to the river, the neighborhood to the east, Bettenhausen, Unterneustadt, Hallenbad Ost, the Platz der Deutschen Einheit, and the church–we realized we needed the place because of its direct connection to the north side. When you cross the river from the north, you can get to Hafenstraße 76 by foot.

TCE What are the documenta fifteen's themes?

RA I wouldn't talk about themes, but rather the seven fundamental values that make up *lumbung*: being locally embedded, humor, generosity, independence, transparency, frugality, and regeneration. There's more to it than you might think: humor, for example, is strategic at its core. It can become a method, a vital lifeline, either in self-defense or as a weapon. Laughter relieves tension. Humor adds a lightness to life and lets us forget, if only briefly, so that we can move on, indeed keep on living.

With the challenges we faced, other aspects and things came to occupy us, like the Fridays for Future movement. For us, it is and was important for us to compare the things that are happening in Kassel with the situation in Jakarta and see what we could draw from our own context to share here.

TCE As you suggested earlier, the starting point for what I would term collectivization was when you merged with Serrum and Grafis Huru Hara to form *Gudskul*. The opportunity for it came from new premises, the former warehouse Gudang in Pancoran, located in the south of Jakarta.

RA Yes, there we use two of the six halls that were offered to us back then. One hall spans 1,000 square meters. Since the area is too huge to run alone, we got the collectives Serrum and Grafis Huru Hara on board. Given their size, the halls were ideal for presenting both our working methods and networks, between eighty and a hundred worldwide, on the occasion of our ten-year anniversary. With our partners, we finally conceived *Gudskul* as a contemporary art *ekosistem* based on friendship, equality, and solidarity, as a space for fostering collaboration and self-organization, for process-based studies, collective practice simulations, critical and experimental learning and sharing. As our base, *Gudskul* has also proven to be a platform of sharing as effective as it is efficient, one that encourages learning processes. It doesn't matter who's occupying it. And it's also possible that in a few years *Gudskul* will only be run by ruangrupa and another collective, while Serrum will have become something else.

TCE How does the platform work?

RA Without rules. We open the tap, let it run, then see what, where, and how things flow. We aren't ingenious enough to formulate anything. In the context of Jakarta, it works perfectly. Because this city spurs you on to grow beyond your dreams. At the same time, it accommodates you so little that it forces you to look around for your own options and solutions. For all the incentives it offers, it makes things hard for you, and that's why we try to pursue everything ourselves, every day, with the help of the *Gudskul ekosistem*. We ask ourselves what is it and what isn't it? How's our security guard doing? What about the woman who sells noodles in our canteen, and the children playing in a friend's studio? It's about interpersonal relationships. Sometimes, when you're tired, you suddenly realize how inattentive you've been to someone.

TCE Within ruangrupa, I don't think there is a fixed division of roles in the sense that one person specializes in this, the other in something else.

RA Yes, by taking care of each other and being transparent about everything, we can fill any gaps. We don't worry about questions like who's going to step in if Andan or Sari can't come to Kassel for some reason, because someone else can take their place. I can do it just as well as anyone else, so Sari doesn't have to ask me or bring it up. Since Iswanto is working with me on the same thing, I could go home early today and he would take on my part, and vice versa. Insofar as the work processes aren't so fixed, each of us can be like a super-sub in football, ready to jump in at various levels. No one performs a task so specialized that it can't be taken over by someone else. Ade may be the one who works out the proposals, but he might also say this time it should be me, Iswanto, or even someone else entirely who doesn't even belong to ruangrupa.

TCE It runs so smoothly because everyone knows about everything and everyone has the same access to resources.

RA Yes, it's our special form of sharing, though it isn't our invention and just a part of Indonesian culture. In Bali, every village has this strong sense of community. They've been building their own system together since they were school children, through alternative education and now through the involvement of tourism, which can also contribute to or influence their needs. In Jakarta, the culture of sharing is no longer as natural. When it happens there, it might take you by surprise. Jakarta is just a huge megacity with more than ten million inhabitants who work hard on various levels, party and, because everything is more expensive than in Bandung, spend a lot of money. But actually, sharing is the traditional way for people to meet each other on the street; it's part of people's self-conception. It's a kind of gesture that comes up again and again. I had to get used to the fact that Jakarta is different from Bandung in that respect. There, I didn't have a dream until I became a father. Suddenly I realized, "Okay, this is how life is, everyone is equal."

THE DECEPTIVE BACKDROPS OF SINGAPORE

TCE What's the reason for the steadily growing number of collectives gaining visibility in recent years? Is it because of the interconnectedness that comes with globalization?

RA Collectives have always existed. Perhaps more so in Asia and South America than in Europe, because the sense of collective belonging is stronger. Your question alludes to the world map of mainstream art, where a collective is marked as soon as it participates in a biennial and thus becomes a player; we aren't interested in that. We're mainly focused on things in Jakarta and don't attach much importance to this form of international recognition. The fact that it's apparently become easier to exist as a collective certainly has to do with the global turn in the art world. The 2021 Turner Prize shortlisted five collectives—including Black Obsidian Sound System (B.O.S.S.), Cooking Sections, Gentle/Radical, and Project Art Works—and finally went to Northern Ireland's Array Collective. By now, "collective" has become a buzzword and increasingly a cliché; everyone brags about working collectively. Maybe this trend will be over in two years.

Over the years, and also now through documenta fifteen, we've discovered so many collectives that we didn't have a clue about before. Unfortunately, we still don't know them too well yet. I'm thinking of Sa Sa Art Projects in Phnom Penh, Cambodia. We didn't know what they were doing until we took a new direction because of our interest in urban topography. We learned that one of our friends is a member of Sa Sa Art Projects, which does a lot for young Cambodian artists and art graduates through creative education programs, exhibitions, their Pisaot artist residency, and other collaborative projects, bolstering dialogue with artists in Asia. I chatted with my friend about their projects and how they work, exist as a space, and what they think about issues like gender. I didn't know anything about Cambodia's history or the Khmer regime. I wanted to know more about it because I had never been to Cambodia. On my first visit to Phnom Penh, I met another friend from Sa Sa Art Projects. Even without being on the world map of art, they enjoy a lot of visibility through their network. They're also participating in documenta. It's similar with Takashi Kuribayashi, who's famous as a solo artist, or with the group Cinema Caravan, which is only active in Zushi, not in Tokyo. They are networked with other friends; we first met them in Arnhem. Their participation in documenta could bring their ideas into global art practice. We care a lot about the success of documenta, sure. But it's more important to us that the "Kassel ekosistem" takes root.

TCE Since you just talked about your trip and time in Phnom Penh, I'd like to take the chance to learn more about the 2011 Singapore Biennale. What was it about?

RA On one hand, it was about questioning the institutions; on the other it was about the place, since Singapore, which was formerly colonized by the British, is a very specific country, or actually just a city. It's far more modern than Indonesia as a society, but also fascist. The main theme was "Open House." *Singapore Fictions* was as much about the Indonesian view of Singapore as it was about challenging Singaporean ideas and attitudes. Because compared to what's allowed in Indonesia, where there's even a red-light district in Jakarta, the situation in Singapore is one of strict regimentation, of censorship, which we were clearly made to feel.

When we proposed setting up a live radio station since there weren't any, it was forbidden. Since what we wanted to do wouldn't work if it wasn't broadcast live, we inevitably gave it up. Doing karaoke or making noise outside in the fields where many Indonesians worked was also prohibited. The alleged laws and policies on noise and against mass gatherings made it impossible. So we decided to do something else and looked for a flea market, which was closed a few years later. Perhaps due to a policy prohibiting street vending. There, we talked to Indonesians from the Melanesian region and bought some stuff related to Singapore in a secondhand store, which we then used in our installation.

One of our fictions was about Singaporean islands, which were part of Malaysia at the time. We imagined an open Singapore. The *Singapore Fictions* we created, some imagined, some based on fact, resided between the political and the social, and were based on the stories of the city's residents, including homeless people, street vendors, migrants, flea market visitors, and all the marginalized people who oppose the government.

We also included a social parody, alluding to a famous female porn star from Singapore who set a world record for having sex with more than 100 men in one day. And this in a country that is outwardly very prude and officially doesn't allow prostitution. We played with this paradox or contradiction between a society that purports to be oh so clean on the outside and what can be discovered and experienced behind the facades. In the 1990s, for example, the Hyatt Hotel seems to have had precisely what was forbidden: porn and prostitutes. Some thought these Singaporean stories were fiction; others believed they were true events.

The stories are also about the relationship between Indonesia and Singapore, the permanent tensions, both historical and political, the competition between Singapore, Indonesia, and Malaysia.

TCE Does it make a difference whether you work in Singapore, São Paulo, or Kassel?

RA In São Paulo, for example, we loved the things that happened at the biennal, and it was wonderful how we lived there. Their body language is different, sometimes they're very direct, like our friends from North Jakarta or North Sumatra. São Paulo has this other atmosphere, which is very pleasant. But the fact that many things are different there also taught us something. And we don't have any problem with that either, because we are always us wherever we go, same thing here in Kassel.

TCE Is it about leaving traces for you?

RA Yes, but it depends on what kind of traces. Visible ones or spiritual ones? The spirit is there. Many of our friends will still refer to ruangrupa even without documenta fifteen; they can still talk about what they experienced from us in practice in different exhibitions. Even in the local context. The Asia Pacific triennial comes to mind as an example. The first time we dealt with it was the seventh edition in 2012, and at the ninth edition I was their advisor. When I came back to Brisbane in 2019, I could experience and see that some of our dear friends had translated the spirits left behind by our triennial into different models. Since the colonial issues, the issues of oppression that we had incorporated into various programs at the 2012 triennial, were still present in the context of Brisbane when I went back there as well as our collective thinking.

If you ask if there are any traces left in Arnhem today, there are some in the form of a landmark or a mural, for sure. But many of the collectives we worked with there didn't stay. Evidently, we couldn't inspire them to keep living and working on site. Instead, they moved to big cities that were promising a better life than in Arnhem.

Anyway, everything we do has different intensities. In 2016 in the Danish Faroe Islands, our presence on site wasn't really grounded, and it was less intense. It was like we'd brought something from Indonesia then showed it in the Listasavn Føroya (Faroe Islands Art Museum) in Tórshavn. The two weeks we spent there weren't an art experience, but a life experience. We were happy to be there, if only because we were the only Indonesians.

TCE Presumably the Western art or cultural world, which usually expects finished artworks, will have some difficulties with documenta's processual *lumbung* practice.

RA We'll see how much negative criticism there'll be about how we handle documenta. For us, the relevant question is whether the seeds will sprout and whether what we plant will continue to grow. I think this documenta demands other forms of reception, reaction, and evaluation.

THE EKOSISTEM'S INGREDIENTS

IN CONVERSATION WITH ISWANTO HARTONO AND REZA AFISINA

TCE Iswanto, when did you join ruangrupa?

IH In 1998 I was working as an architect, and I joined ruangrupa in 2008.

RA On July 27, 1997 we were directly confronted with the political situation for the first time.

IH Yes, when the New Order crushed the Democratic Party.

RA There was a clash between the supporters of the major parties, and the Indonesian Dance Festival was also being held at that time. And that's how we knew Iswanto as a professional artist; we liked his works. Then, when we moved into a new house, we thought we needed more ingredients for various projects we were involved with. So in 2008 we approached Iswanto to ask him to join our *Arts Laboratory, ArtLab* for short. We called it *ArtLab* because we didn't just want to focus on artist residencies, but also on longer and sustainable projects. For this we needed ingredients and inspiration, from Iswanto, for example, or others we knew. He and Andan were the only ones who joined us during that time. The natural way of working together was the one suggested with the image of cooking, namely putting together different ingredients as part of our recipes. At the time, there were many so-called ruangrupa families, some of whom did not continue working with us for various reasons. Either because they were looking for other work opportunities, or because they aspired to their own careers. We always say that we don't just want to grow as a space, but as people. The space can be small by all means. The main thing is that we grow. We made ourselves part of Jakarta's center. In addition to working closely together, based on our shared artistic practices, it was important for us to have our own space to question, evaluate, and also criticize our previous work.

In 2010, we had conversations about how to survive as an art collective in our context. Other collectives that collaborated closely with us in Jakarta were in a similar situation; they had to deal with the same problems. We had to rent a house, submit an application every two years, write a rcport, and develop programs. Some of these tasks overlapped, so as friends we thought up a strategy together about how to share our resources and convince funders to see us as one big *ekosistem*, rather than ruangrupa with this amount and Serrum with another. This was how we worked together, but not as effectively as we would have liked. Therefore, we also thought about a model for economic circulation, that is, how to generate collective power to express and spread our experiences. All in all, a very experimental way of approaching things. Fortunately, Serrum, one of the groups closest to pedagogy at the only art school in Jakarta, were able to formulate our experiences into a curriculum, which is now one of the topics taught at *Gudskul*. We decided to sketch out the resources we had at our disposal: materials, money, equipment, funding

WE SEE LUMBUNG AS A PRINCIPLE FOR COOPERATION, BASED ON GENEROSITY AND EMPATHY. SUSTAINABILITY IS ONLY GUARANTEED WHEN RESOURCES ARE CONTINUOUSLY RENEWED AND REPLENISHED.

WE LIVE IN JAKARTA NEAR THE CILIWUNG AND LOVE THE RIVER FLOWING PAST. SINCE KASSEL LIVES WITH THE FULDA, WE THOUGHT WHY NOT ACTIVATE THE RIVER.

systems. After the Jakarta Biennale in 2015, we found ourselves together in the 6,000 sqare meters space of a former warehouse for the first time. This time was a big challenge. Firstly, because we had been selected as the curatorial collective for the *SONSBEEK '16: transACTION* in Arnhem, and secondly, because just maintaining the huge space was a lot of work. We took care of a lot of other things at the same time, which was quite exhausting. At first, we didn't think we needed a big space. Around 2016, we finally considered acquiring our own with the help of a bank loan. At the exact same moment, we were unexpectedly granted a rather large amount of money for projects and asked the sponsors if we could use the funds to support our infrastructure, for example, by buying a plot of land or a house. Because in terms of programming, we were an ensemble of three collectives–alongside Serrum and Grafis Huru Hara–and had a lot to do. In this way, we promoted trust in our network, and successfully so. We bought our own space from the grant. It was only 700 square meters, and because we couldn't build anything on the property, we set up containers, and that still works today.

TCE What is *ArtLab* exactly?

IH *ArtLab* serves as a kind of kitchen to deepen research in the field of art related to urban and social issues, but also to aesthetic approaches. A platform that serves to put our projects up for debate.

RA With *ArtLab* we created our own showcase, so to speak, for ruangrupa projects. In a research project that dealt with unconventional design, for example, we collected designs created by ordinary people in villages or cities wherever.

TCE Why did you want to join ruangrupa?

IH In Indonesia there are four major art cities; apart from Jakarta, there's also Yogyakarta, Bandung, and Denpasar. These cities are quite different, and Jakarta is the most difficult of all. The cost of living is high, and their sprawl makes it hard to get together.

That is, unless you meet in a small place like the art college. The fact that the cities mentioned have art colleges means that there are corresponding communities. I didn't belong to any of them, nor did I have many artist friends when I was working as an architect. Although I attended art school at the same time as Reza, we never ran into each other for the first two years. Eventually I was a scholarship student in India, where I studied urban planning, and when I returned I didn't continue going to school, but worked as an artist. When I had the opportunity to meet ruangrupa, I was delighted to join them. Because Indonesia was suffering from strong social tensions, racial and religious conflicts, and ruangrupa was absolutely free of them at that time, and of course still is: it's all a big mix, very lively, diverse, and dynamic, there aren't any limits. I felt accepted and comfortable. It becomes clear why, given my personal and family background. I come from a diasporic Chinese family. The regime took advantage of the self-inflicted tensions and the fact that the Indonesian Communist Party was one of the largest in the world in terms of membership during the 1940s and 1950s, along with the Russian and Chinese Communist Parties. During the first regime under Sukarno, who had been president since independence in 1945, Indonesia maintained very good relations with China, Russia, and the Eastern Bloc through the Communist Party of Indonesia, which had a pragmatic relationship to the government. The USA supported the coup to overthrow the regime because of its closeness to China and Russia. General Suharto exploited these circumstances while blaming the Communist Party for initiating the coup. He thus tried to legitimize the genocide of Communist Party members and sympathizers, as well as citizens of Chinese origin, which was carried out until 1966. Some five or four million people were killed for no reason, others imprisoned. All Chinese names were forbidden; everyone had to change theirs. Although born in Indonesia, I had to show my birth certificate as proof of my Indonesian citizenship. There were massive restrictions preventing the Chinese community from serving in the government, the army, the police; they were treated as inferior people. These tensions persisted until 1998.

CRAMMED INTO SOUTH JAKARTA AND THE PRINCIPLE OF FERMENTATION

TCE Earlier, you spoke of ingredients, the ingredients that ruangrupa hoped you would have. What role do they play?

RA We've always said that part of our art-making process is that we never consider ingredients to be wrong. We allow for mistakes because we learn through experience. That's what we call fermentation. The results can be surprising, like kimchi or pickles. There are no wrong ingredients, except for allergens, which you should probably avoid. In a certain sense, we've been fermenting ruangrupa since the beginning, cherishing and nurturing it. We don't shy away from confrontation, nor do we have a problem facing many things, especially things that happened earlier, for example, the conditions at the college, because what we care about is growing. In this growth process, there's always something grotesque that we have to accept. Producing it isn't failure in any way, because it is part of the process of growth.

Even if we take care of documenta fifteen as a big family, we don't know if it is already growing. We have to nurture, cultivate, and harvest the seeds that arrive in Kassel. But we never thought about which exact ingredients we need. We accept things even if they aren't always ideal for us because we've been evaluating ourselves from the beginning. That's very different for us than for many other collectives.

We loved Yogyakarta. Living there is perfect for someone who wants to work as an artist. Living in Jakarta, you can observe things and learn from what's happening in this juggernaut. They're our daily ingredients. Can you imagine that every time we wake up and look at the street, there are sixteen million people and six million motorcycles on the road? This city is our inspiration, it's always different. Not only the politics, but also the climate, the trash, the floods, and the urban development, everything just seems different every time. If close friends from other parts of the city didn't keep us up to do date, sometimes we wouldn't even know what was going on in the north, east or south of the city, since we're crammed into South Jakarta.

IH Like Reza says, it isn't about right or wrong ingredients, because we don't have members, and that's exactly why Reza and Ade didn't ask me, "Do you want to become a member of ruangrupa?" but rather, "Do you feel like participating in a project?" Thus, a natural selection takes place. You can come if you like it and leave if it doesn't work for you.

TCE What has shaped ruangrupa's collective practice the most?

IH One thing that strengthened and expanded our knowledge was dealing with the way the political situation influences collective practice. Today, Indonesia has neither a very strong left, nor a very strong right. The right is stronger than the left because it is dominated by the religious right, and the left has been greatly weakened since the events of 1965. The second thing we learned was the values we associated with our *lumbung* practice. When we addressed these, we already knew that the art shared a universal vision through our experience of working with others. There are commonalities, especially sharing, which is what *lumbung* is based on.

TCE What are the major changes ruangrupa experienced over the years?

IH One change happened in 2015 with the launch of the interdisciplinary cultural platform *Gudang Sarinah Ekosistem*, which aims to create an integrated support system for creative talents, communities, and institutions, with networks that share knowledge and ideas, promote critical thinking, creativity, and innovation.

The idea for *Gudang Sarinah Ekosistem* also came to us because in 2015, we were offered two of six halls of the former one-hectare Gudang Sarinah warehouse in Pancoran. One hall covers 1,000 square meters. The area was too large to run on our own. We didn't have enough or the necessary personnel. We also lacked the energy and time. That's why we got the collectives Serrum and Grafis Huru Hara on board. With them, we conceived *Gudskul*, an educational platform with a pedagogical model that focuses on collective learning and building a grassroots *ekosistem* to create an infrastructure for Indonesia's contemporary art scene. We networked as a collective from the very beginning. It was like a chain reaction triggered by Ade's network.

Through *Gudskul*, that is, through this intercollective expansion, ruangrupa dissolves to a certain extent in a narrower sense, and with the additional expansion of the platform to include more collectives, artists, for documenta fifteen, we are pushing this dissolution even further.

TCE The collectives are as diverse as the individuals within them. Does the concept of group subjectivity mean anything to you?

IH I don't know. documenta's invitation to ruangrupa was addressed to the whole group, and what will be shown on the opening day isn't an assemblage of individual works, nor is it an assemblage of Reza's work and mine. We've been working together closely to produce a single work that testifies to the fact that it comes from all of us. It is something completely different from a combination of diverse individual works that can be separated.

RA It is something new without any traces leading back to me or Iswanto in a way where you could say, "This is typical Iswanto and this is typical Reza." Within the collective ideas, this is also difficult for us, because we know the character and qualities of our dear friends from ground up. Growing up at the same time, we've had similar, though different backgrounds as a result of our relationships to our families, cultures, and the particular ethnic groups we belong to. I'm Sundanese, Iswanto Javanese, Andan Bugis, Ade a mix of Sundanese and Javanese, and Indra a cross between Madurese and Sundanese. Between these, there is a lot to share, and that's one thing. Secondly, going back to the feeling that we are like a family: we can rely on each other for our basic needs.

The first time we engaged in group exhibitions and delivered something as a collective, that involved our working relationships and process, was when we got the invitation to the Gwangju Biennale in South Korea in 2002. Not yet two years together at the time, there were many internal issues to resolve. We questioned the space and how we could fill it, ideally in relation to our context, and with which artists. It wasn't conceptual because we also wanted to see how others would see a space in the context of the biennial and use it for their own needs. UNESCO gave us an award for our efforts. Since it wasn't the first time we had gotten quite a lot of money and had also won other awards before, we thought we could make that our basic structure for the purpose of paying a monthly salary. That was the beginning of our economy.

Over the years, we were often confronted with our poverty. For example, we went without payment for six months in 2004, but fortunately we were able to continue the programs on our premises without problems with the rent. Then, in 2008 we didn't get paid for more than eight months, and the owner urged us to pay back the arrears. During that time, some of us already had a family to support. It wasn't the only job. Iswanto had his own architecture office and I had a job at a company, but most of the time we worked in ruangrupa. So we didn't mind walking this financially difficult path together, and we developed different strategies to do so.

IH Yes, even though we're all artists in ruangrupa, we don't live from selling our works. We're outside the capitalist art market. There are only a few works in the collection of the embassy in Qatar, and if I'm not mistaken Ade's work is represented in some museum collections, but we don't live from that. Indra Ameng is into music and a DJ. Ade hired himself out to the a company. I occasionally make money from architecture or as an exhibition designer. So we're far away from the art market, and that's also because the situation in Jakarta is different from Yogyakarta and Bandung, which have booming industries. There, most artists profit from the art market. If a museum were to buy one of our works, no one from ruangrupa would claim a right to a percentage of the money. As agreed, it goes into the collective pot. The question of ownership is completely irrelevant to us.

INDIVIDUALLY OR COLLECTIVELY?

TCE It wasn't common to work collectively as artists in Indonesian art schools.

IH It'd be worth talking to Ade about that, because he was one of ruangrupa's initiators. After thirty years of repression, it was important to have a small space where you could express yourself in this sprawling city, which was impossible before. That's one thing. The second is that Ade came up with the idea for ruangrupa right after the Rijksakademie. What I know from him is that he was very much oriented towards Western studio practice in Amsterdam. Working individually in a studio, he realized that this didn't work for him at all; he longed for a space where he didn't have to work alone. The fact that people work individually at art schools in Indonesia probably stems from the fact that art education there was taken over from Holland during the colonial period. In other words, collective art practice was not common. After the fall of the regime, everything came at once, so many NGOs were formed, especially in politics, but also in art. Back in Jakarta, Ade felt the contrast or contradiction between the individual and the collective in view of global changes. For the Indonesian context, the desire for a space with friends immediately after Suharto's rule was very timely.

TCE What is the difference between what's generated individually and what's generated collectively?

RA It never occurred to us, nor were we ever forced to single out what one person or another did versus what we did collectively, because we inspire each other and trust in our process. Those were our basic ingredients. Many of our friends joined ruangrupa in the beginning in the mistaken

Opening of the *Ok. Video Festival*, 2003

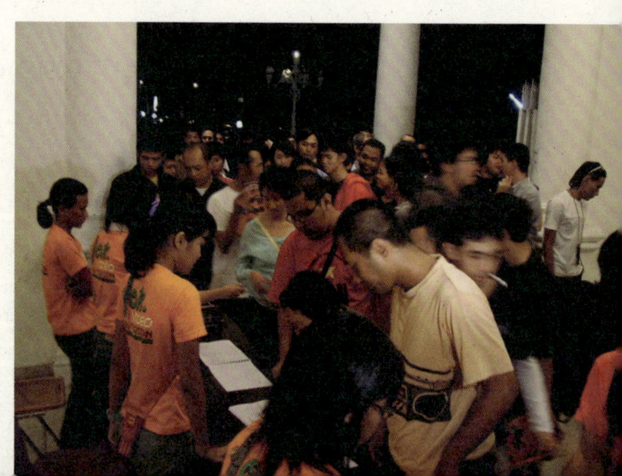

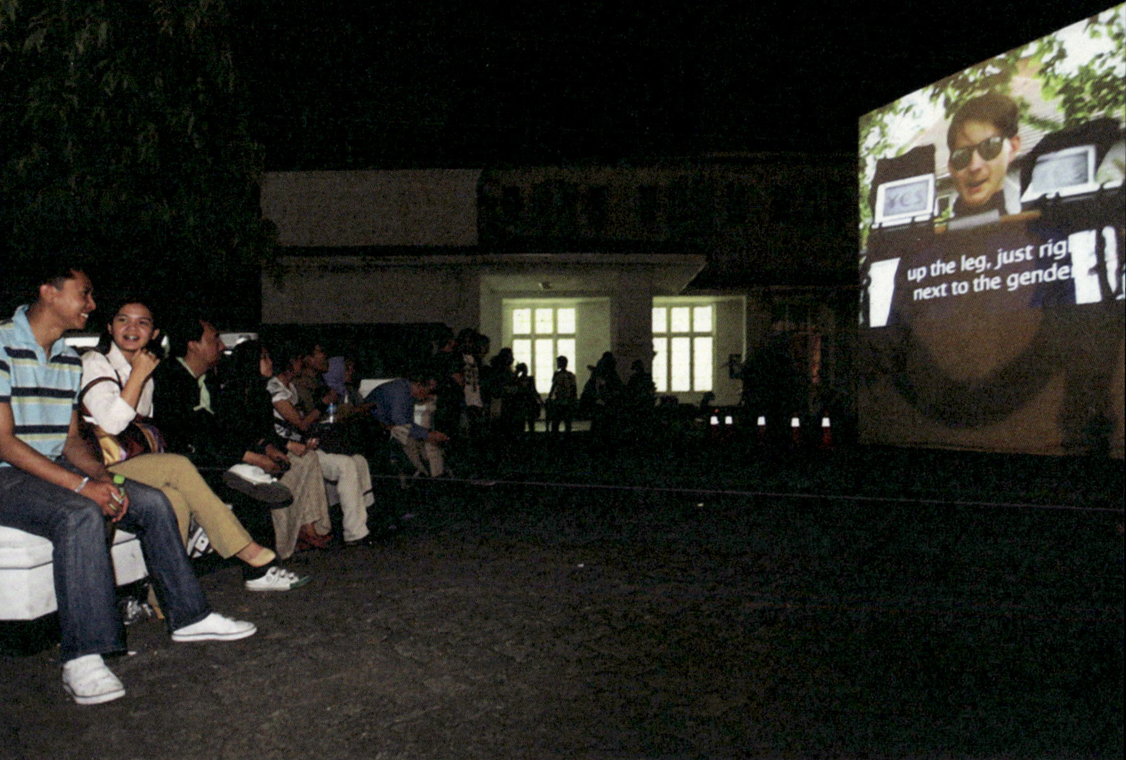

Premier of the *Ok. Video - Jakarta International Video Art Festival*, 2003

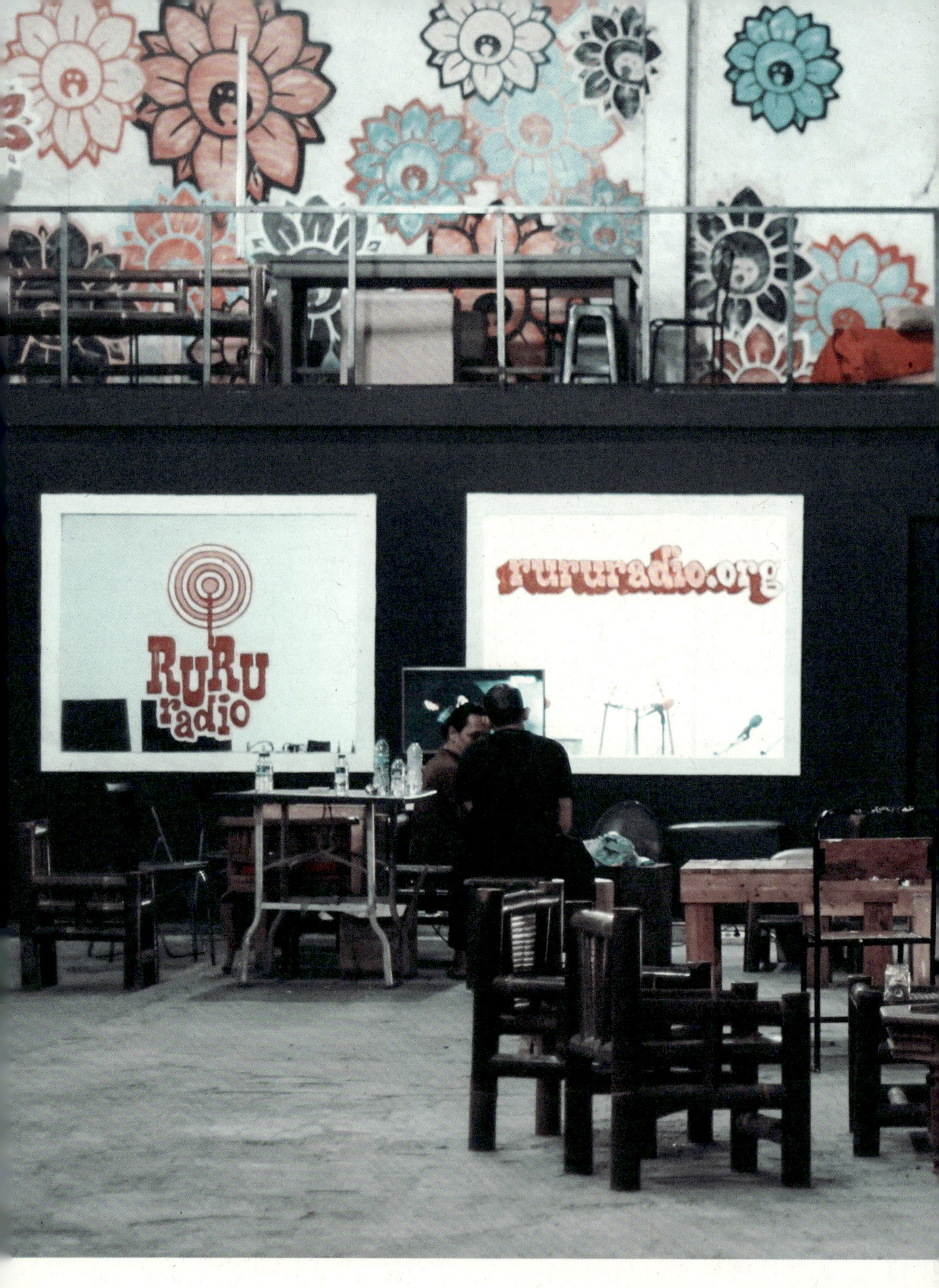
RuRu radio
rururadio.org

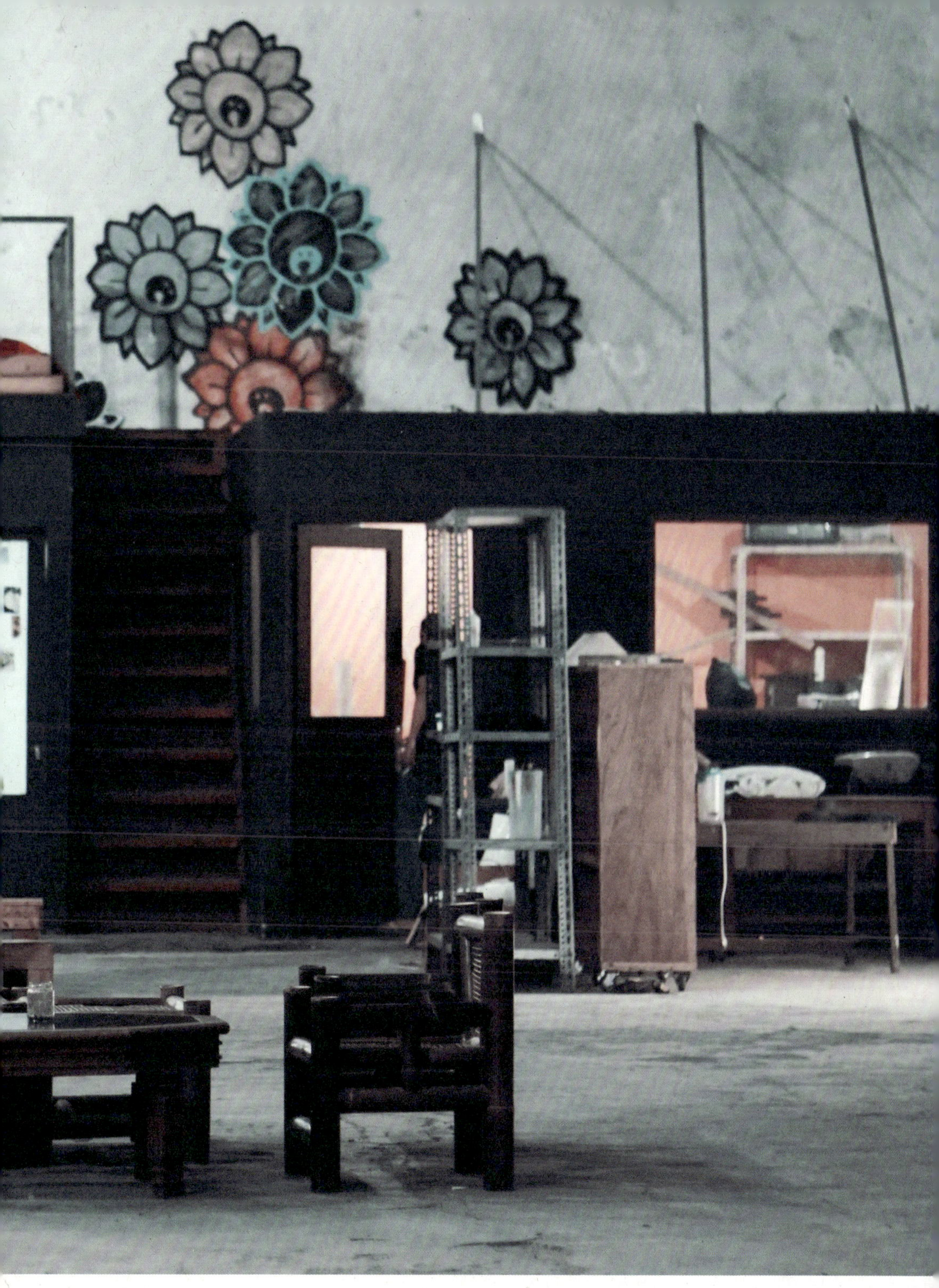

RURUradio is an online streaming radio run by artists and interdisciplinary creatives to discuss current issues people facing in Jakarta.

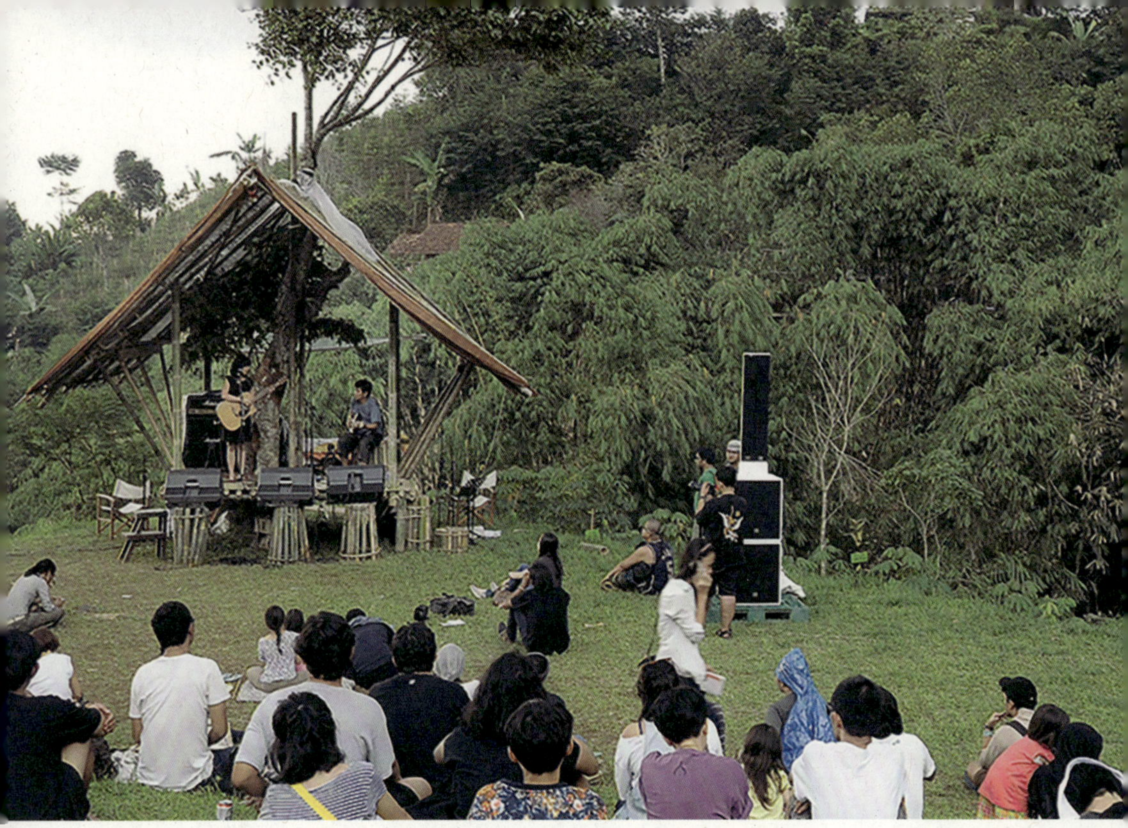

RRREC fest, West Java, 2019

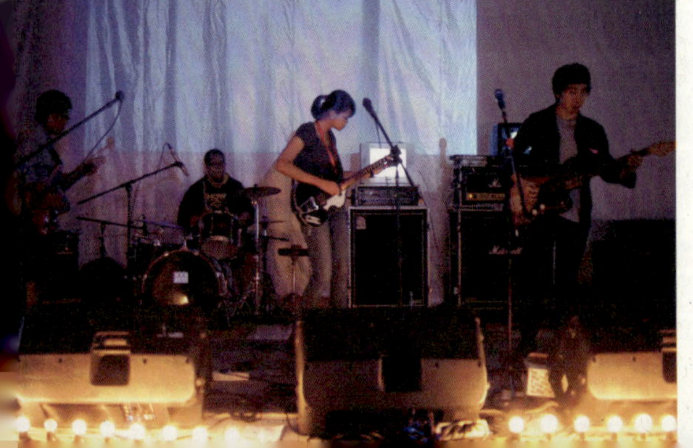

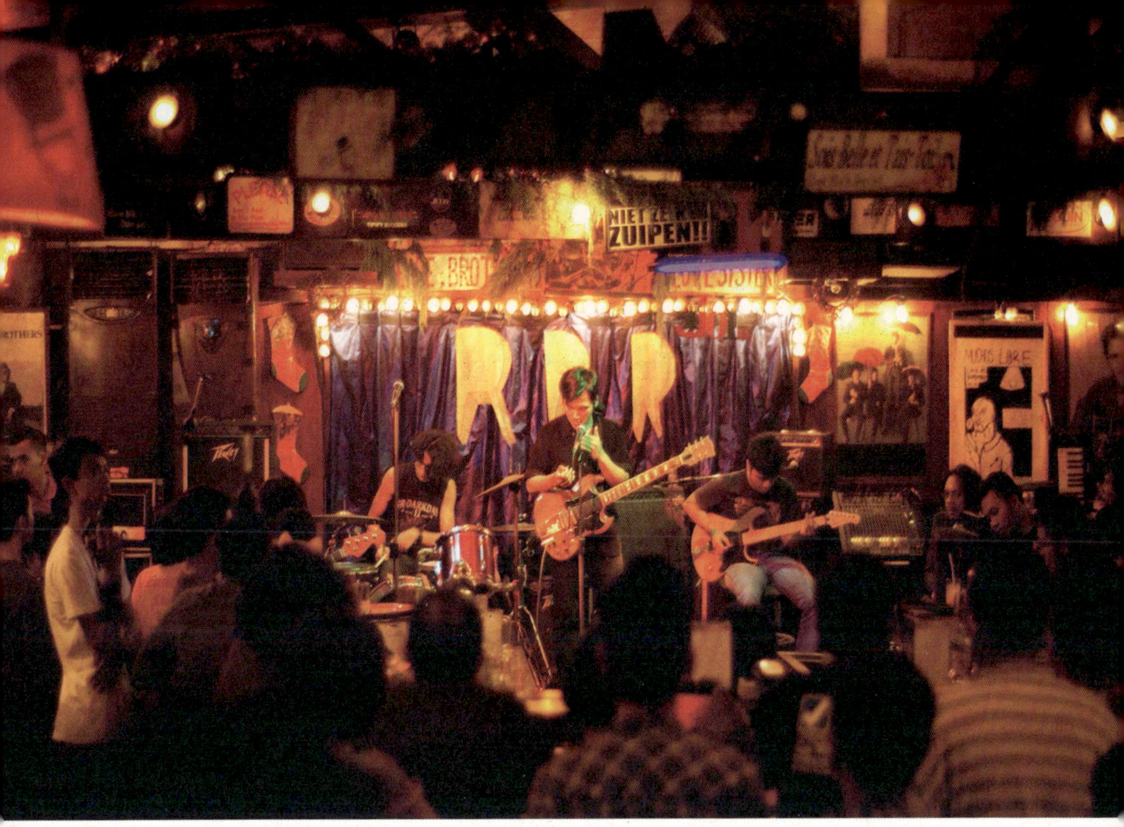
ZUIPEN!!

hope that we would be good for their careers. They joined ruangrupa for either economic or publicity reasons, or just for coolness. But most of them failed. I mean, failed in the sense that they suddenly felt they shouldn't continue with ruangrupa. But it wasn't that they left because they didn't get any money from us. Because we never talked about money, not even when we asked Iswanto if he was interested in our project, because we were interested in him and wanted to share some of his ingredients with others. "Why not?" he answered, without asking if he would get a salary or if the funding had already been secured. It's about trust. But of course we did have a fund for it.

Before Andan approached us in 2007, he worked in a large organization that supported the arts. He said he liked spending time with us and asked whether we had a job or something for him to do. "Why? You have a good job," I challenged him. "Yes, but it doesn't satisfy my needs." Instead of money, he talked about the possibility of working together.

TCE Shifting gears: There was already some talk about censorship of the live radio station at the Singapore Biennale. What actually prompted you to found *RURUradio*?

RA There are a lot of radio communities in Indonesia. Radio has been really popular and it's significance for us is that we grew up with it. Running our own radio station appealed to us because our taste in music is very different. Sometimes at karaoke, we'd say, "Why don't we combine this?" A colleague who organized karaoke parties for companies and events is now the main producer of *RURUradio*. He created this open source digital radio platform for us. At that time, there were only 150 listeners. As soon as we did it digitally, listening to radio became cool. We asked people for their playlists, arranged it, and created a program for listeners by asking them if they wanted to talk about how to survive in Jakarta. At that time, we didn't have a fee structure, we just offered airtime while listeners could have their own music played, without fixed times or commercials. In a nutshell, *RURUradio* is an online streaming radio with artists and interdisciplinary creatives discussing everyday problems of people in the city of Jakarta.

TCE farid told us he was a fan of punk. How are the different music genres reflected in your radio station?

RA Just so you know, Indra is a band manager and the one most closely connected to Jakarta's music scene. Earlier, in the 1990s, he managed an indie Britpop band. Sometimes Ade would organize music events in the east of Jakarta with his friends, combining skate rock, street culture, and BMX, and I used to play in a band occasionally. So we had a certain relationship with music, which was also part of our everyday work when we founded ruangrupa. For the seventh edition of the Asia Pacific Triennial of Contemporary Art in Brisbane, we faked the archive of an Indonesian underground punk band from the 1970s, building a bridge between Jakarta and Brisbane, where there was also a strong punk rock movement from 1975 to 1984.

TCE What is your collective practice like, actually? More spontaneous than deliberate?

RA We proceed more spontaneously and impulsively than according to plan. This is also because we don't want to centralize everything in the context of our artistic practice, because each individual is a part of the resource and determines whether their own is suitable for sharing. We've always said, "Give without expecting anything in return!" When we connect intercollective collaboration, i.e. the *ekosistem*, to our artistic practice because we are artists, it doesn't imply that we want to impose it on others. On the contrary, we hope to take in the things happening around us, not only in the broader context of Jakarta, but also in our small neighborhood there. Since it is part of our resources, we also want to give something back to it.

Just as documenta is a resource for us, ruangrupa is a resource for documenta. It has nothing to do with generosity, which involves giving away something you own. It's like we have something in common that we share. We're convinced that we can learn from the documenta and that the exchange of resources will be beneficial to us as Indonesians and take us further. Likewise, we hope that documenta will enrich "Kassel's ekosistem."

TCE Sharing seems like it's part of your flesh and blood. How did you experience this culture of sharing in the family?

IH Sometimes I think my family isn't as perfect at this as ruangrupa is. (laughs)

RA And occasionally it's quite complicated.

IH I come from a normal family. In some places like the Sunda Islands, where extended families are very close, the cohesion is even stronger. The extended family is also very important to Chinese people. My mother has a family with twelve brothers and sisters, and my grandmother is the heart of the family. If someone doesn't have money to buy food or whatever, they share. When everyone starts doing that, it can get to be a bit too much, but sharing is a kind of value everywhere in Indonesia. In our neighborhood workspace, we share money with each other every month. Five of us put aside, say, 100 every week, and we roll the dice every month so you get the pot and can buy something, and the next time it's Reza, etc. We also take care of neighborhood security collectively. Today you do the night watch, and tomorrow I'll do it.

THE PASSION FOR VIDEO

TCE Your music or video festivals are also a form of sharing, in this case of experiences in particular, and moreover interactions with the audience. How did the *Ok. Video – Jakarta International Video Art Festival* come about?

RA For the festival, before we started it, we had to focus on the necessities of creating this artistic process. New media and the contemporary art scene in Jakarta were closely linked to the audiovisual in the form of video culture. Jakarta is a mega-city with capital and industry, home to many wealthy families who had a strong interest in pushing audiovisual culture forward, with reels of film, VHS or Betamax, and getting involved in this field was more natural to us than getting involved in contemporary painting, insofar as none of us were trained as painters. Furthermore, one of our dear friends who was part of the network at the Rijksakademie came to Jakarta and introduced us to what he called video art. I studied cinematography and was mostly familiar with so-called film noir, since at the time, only French and American film was on the faculty's curriculum. And as a student, everyone had their preferences, depending on their attitude towards the two countries. I spontaneously liked video art, and the question was: how should we approach the medium, how to challenge the ideas about method, and how to be strategic? We needed a solid foundation, a project, and not just short screenings in the hope of getting feedback from viewers. So the *Ok. Video – Jakarta International Video Art Festival* was created in 2004 as a biennal and was held every two years until 2017.

At the same time, since 2000, that is, after the New Order regime, discussions had been sparked about what public space is, and we were also asking this question. For us, knowledge about public space meant engaging with it by holding activities like the festival in Jakarta. We answered the question about what a public space is by creating a forum for people to celebrate together, even if they didn't have a clue about video art. At least they could come together and have fun at the National Gallery of Indonesia as a landmark.

We also looked at the College Student Forum of Jakarta. We thought, why don't we create a space where many students can come to initiate something, have visual experiences, or if they want, contribute their artistic skills. People only ever talk about art in the context of art schools. But we know that artistic things–be it music, photographs, drawings, performances, etc–are also done by people who haven't been to an academy. So we questioned this idea of how art is created. In the first four years of ruangrupa, we acquired experiences with the reception of visual things that come with the idea of big cities. We tried to represent and articulate these, and thought the younger generation might have their own ideas about how to approach or bring in questions about visual experiences, not just in terms of artistic space. We learned from our friends at art school that many of them were just doing art in order to formally complete their studies. We thought it was unfortunate. They were obviously different from us, who provoked their teachers with questions. "Why should I paint or make a film?" For me, cinematography was just an entry point; I could make a film just as well as anything else. It was a permanent challenge unlike the young students who were only doing something because they'd been asked to. So we wanted to get them out of the framework of art school and give them time to exchange with others. I mean, the festival was just as an excuse to have more adequate conversations and focus on the phenomena of visual culture. That's always better than listening to lectures.

TCE What was your particular interest in video?

RA It was that most of us liked watching movies. Moreover, we were thinking about the new possibilities for producing our own films at home instead of going to the cinema, and we felt like looking into so-called video art practices in the Indonesian context. As for the College Student Forum, it was only held in Jakarta. We felt that Yogyakarta should set up its own forum, because of local differences and because the experiences that students share there are necessarily different from those in Jakarta.

TCE Part of your practice is cooperating with other collectives, not only for documenta fifteen. What's the goal of this network of collectives?

RA We don't only work with collectives. The difference is this: if you work only with a single artist, you only meet one person. But if you cooperate with a collective, you might make not just one friend, but maybe even two. Moreover, it's more fun and entertaining to sit and eat at the same table with many people. You see many happy faces around you and hear what the food tastes like for others.

TCE ruangrupa doesn't have a concept in the strict sense, but the idea of being together.

RA Yes, in general you can say that. I already drew the comparison to the methodology of football. It's about positioning and how to keep the ball moving within the framework of rules and definitions, and how to communicate with each other on the field as a team.

TCE What are your main concerns for your documenta?

RA First and foremost, it's about the experience. documenta isn't just an exhibition; it also accommodates different platforms, and so we're also inviting ourselves to experience works or what other collectives are dealing with.

TCE Are you ever afraid of losing yourself in something foreign or in others?

IH No, because working with others, experiencing other cultural practices, especially collective art practices strengthens our understanding of both how we and other collectives function. They feed off each other and broaden our collective perspective. I think we have come out of things stronger for having worked in other places and cities like São Paulo, Singapore, or here in Europe.

TCE Aren't you worried that documenta might make you too established on the global art market?

IH We discussed this once.

TCE.: Only once?

IH Yes, we think that despite Turner Prize, it hasn't necessarily gotten any easier to exist as a collective today, possibly not even after documenta.

WE ALWAYS SAY THAT WE DON'T JUST WANT TO GROW AS A SPACE, BUT AS PEOPLE. THE SPACE CAN BE SMALL BY ALL MEANS. THE MAIN THING IS THAT WE GROW.

WE ALLOW FOR MISTAKES BECAUSE WE LEARN THROUGH EXPERIENCE. THAT'S WHAT WE CALL FERMENTATION. THE RESULTS CAN BE SURPRISING LIKE KIMCHI OR PICKLES.

IT NEVER OCCURRED TO US, NOR WERE WE EVER FORCED TO SINGLE OUT WHAT ONE PERSON OR ANOTHER DID VERSUS WHAT WE DID COLLECTIVELY, BECAUSE WE INSPIRE EACH OTHER AND TRUST IN OUR PROCESS. THOSE WERE OUR BASIC INGREDIENTS.

PEOPLE ONLY EVER TALK ABOUT ART IN THE CONTEXT OF ART SCHOOLS.
BUT WE KNOW THAT ARTISTIC THINGS – BE IT MUSIC, PHOTOGRAPHS, DRAWINGS, PERFORMANCES, ETC – ARE ALSO DONE BY PEOPLE WHO HAVEN'T BEEN TO AN ACADEMY.

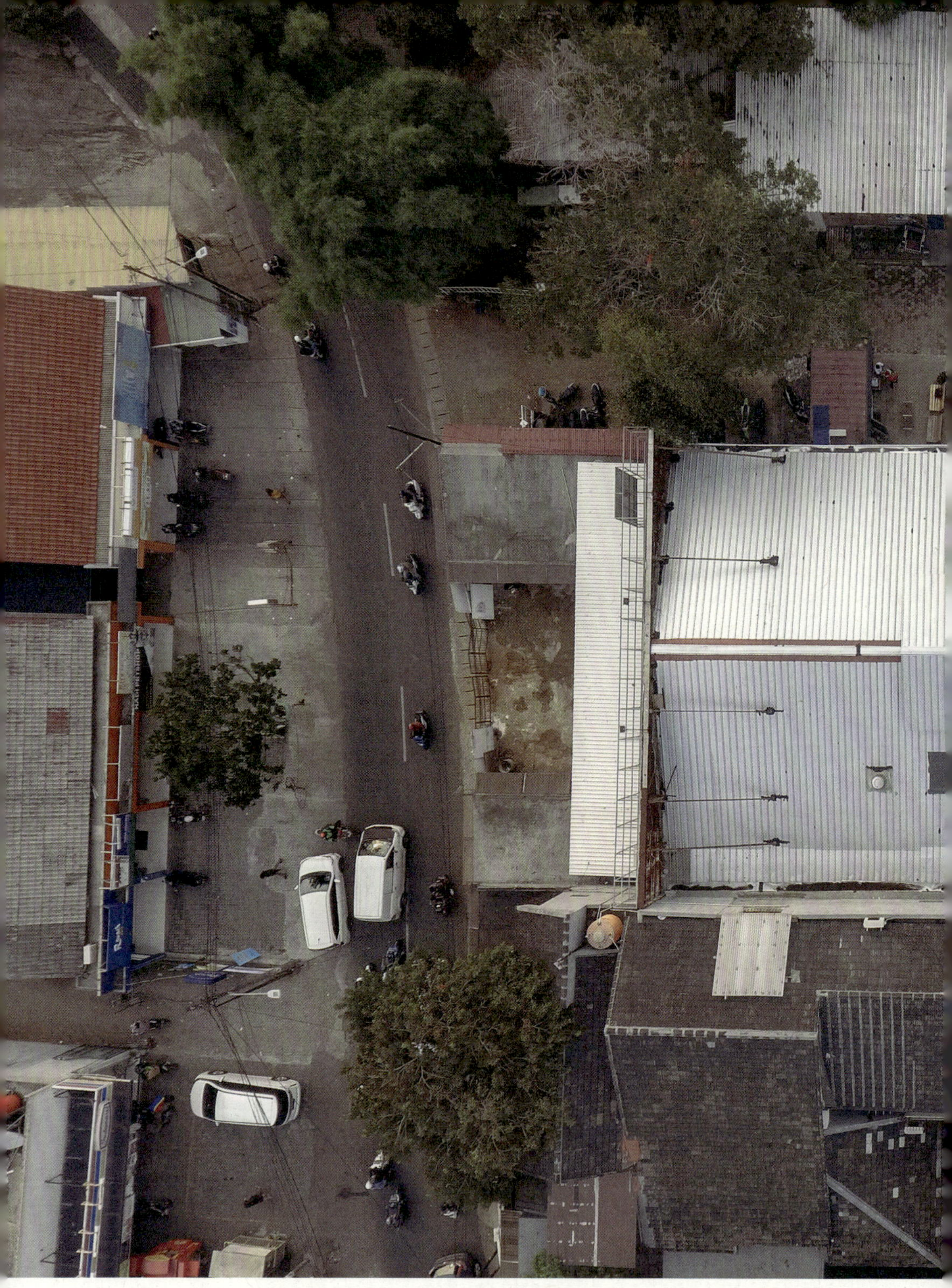

Gudskul covers 2,000 square meters

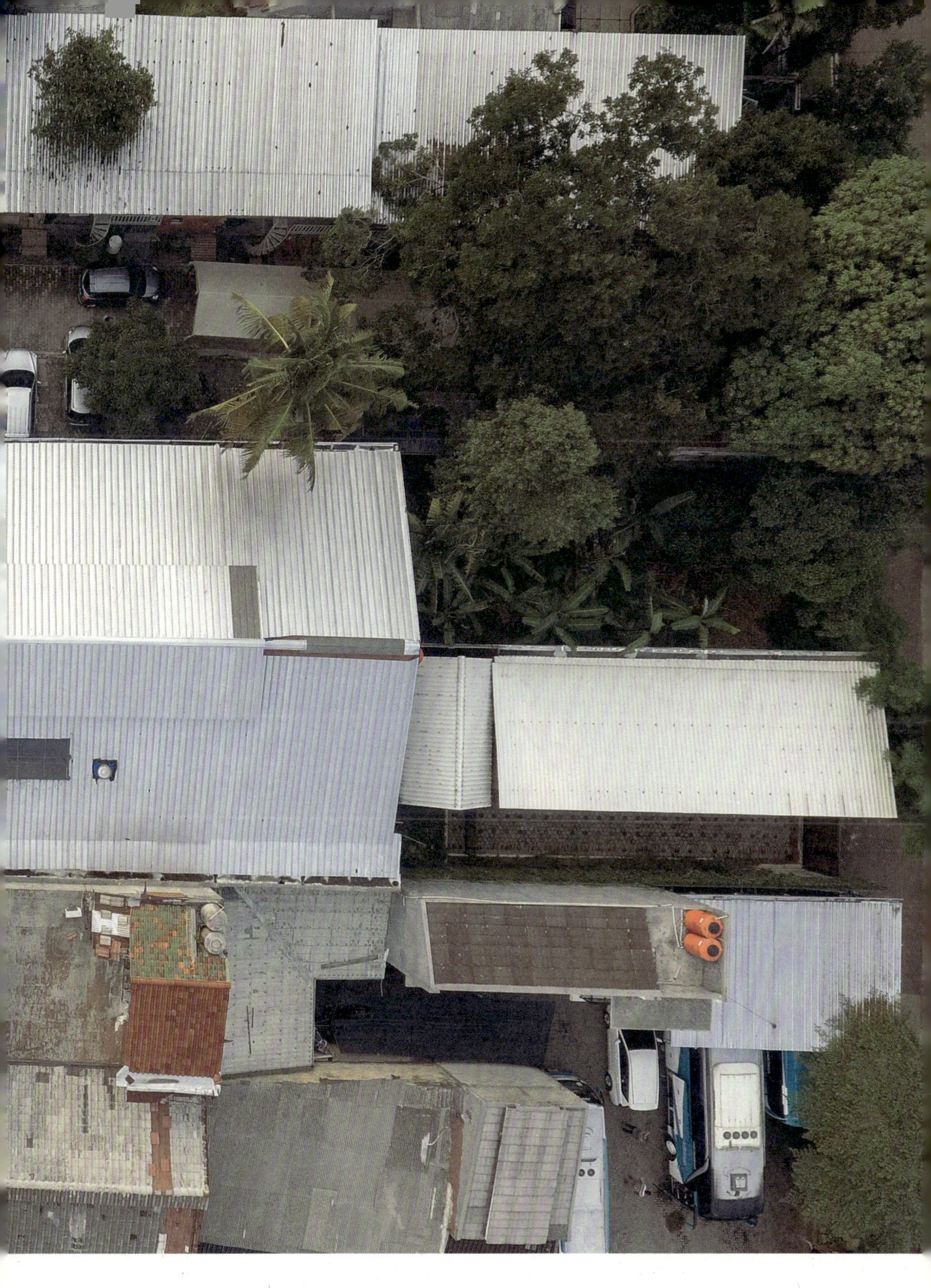

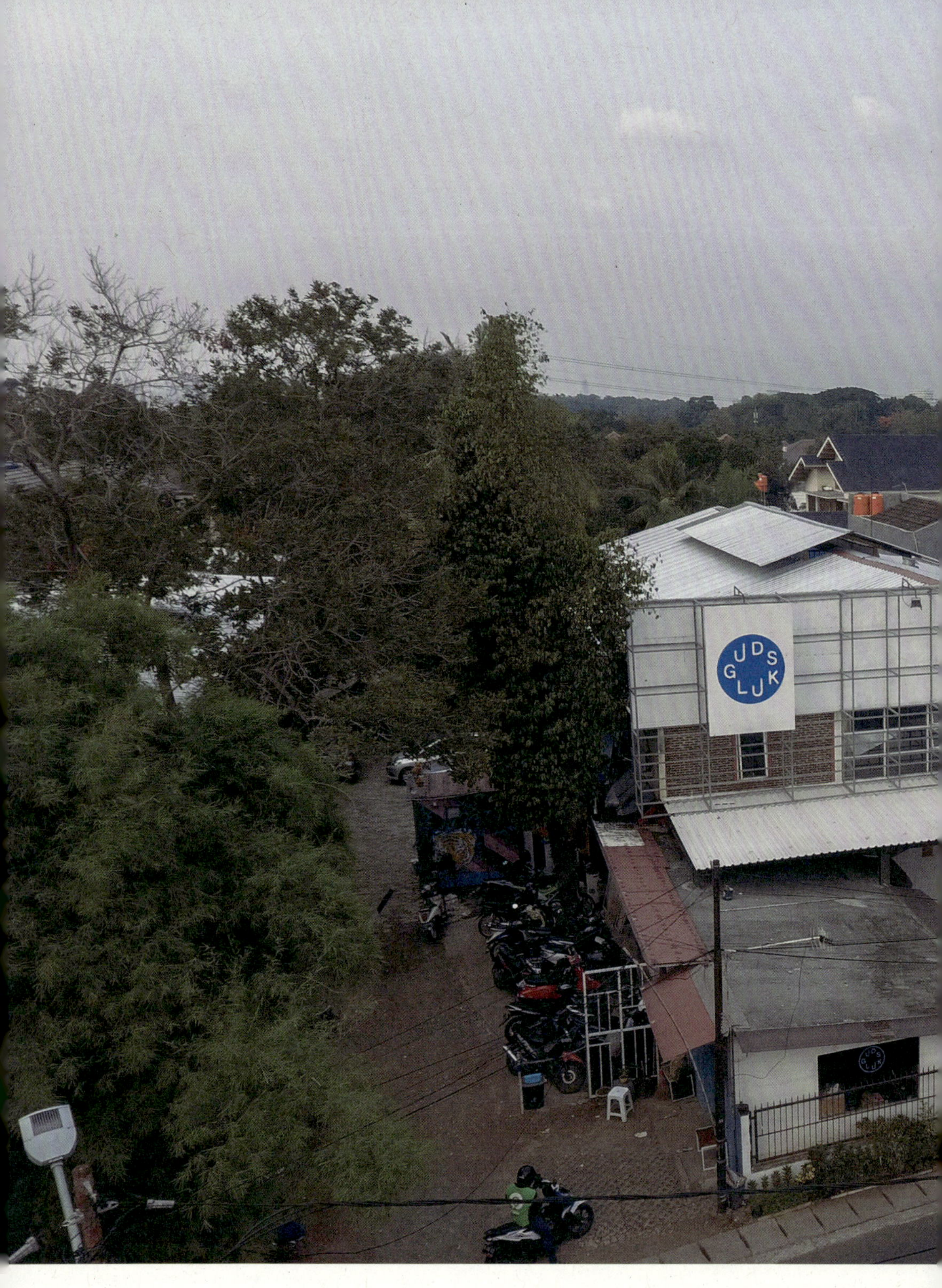
GUDSKLU

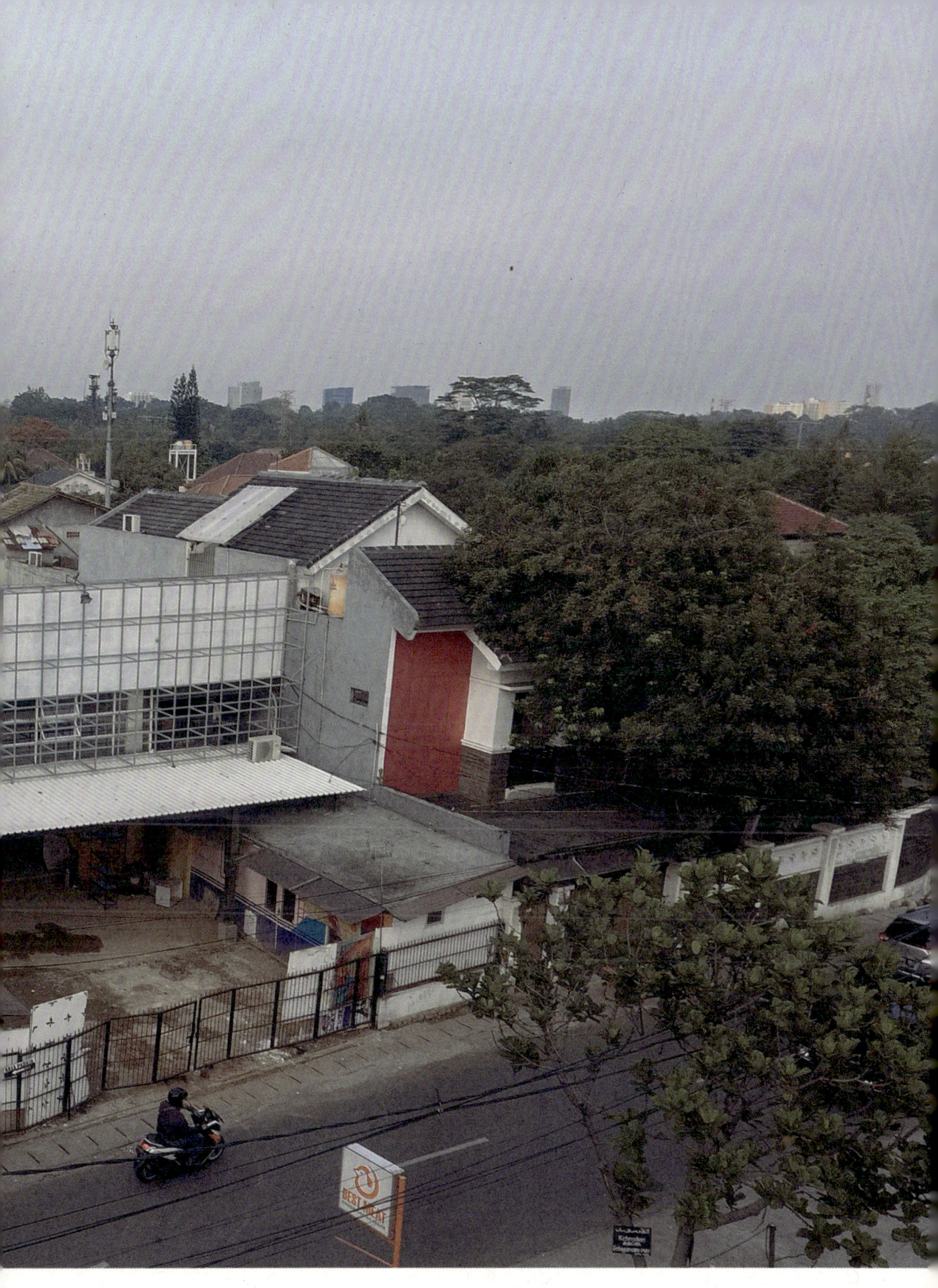

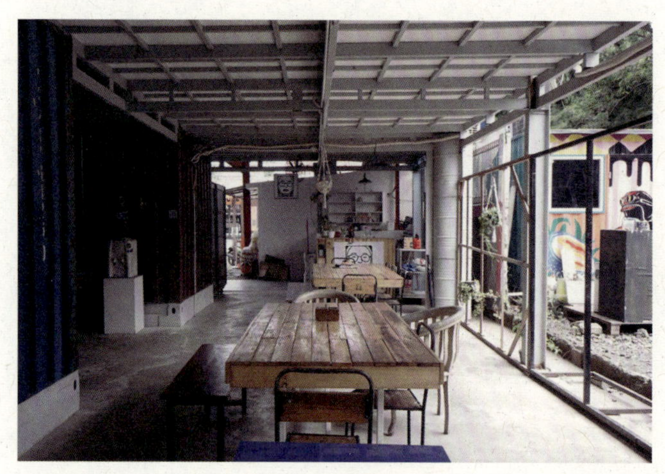

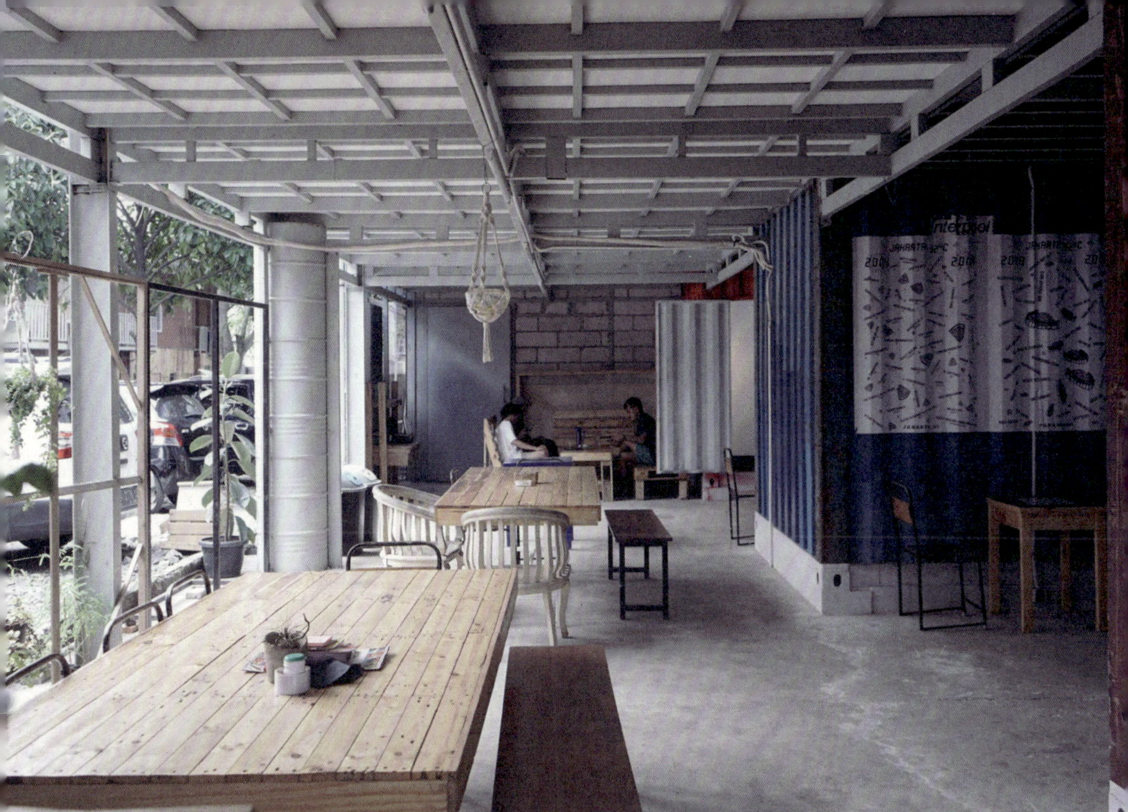

Gudskul is home to the workspaces of ruangrupa and the two other collectives as well as the *RURU Gallery* and the *Jakarta 32°C* student network.

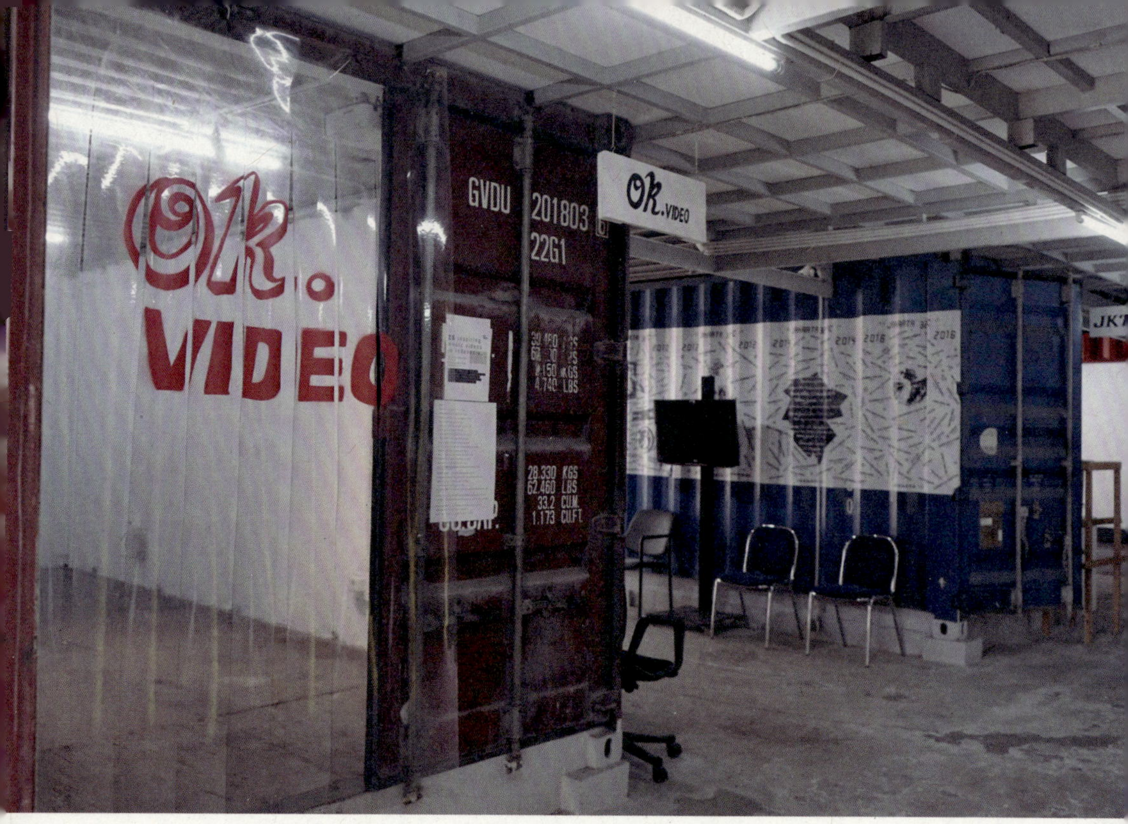

Freight containers form the spatial layout of *Gudskul*

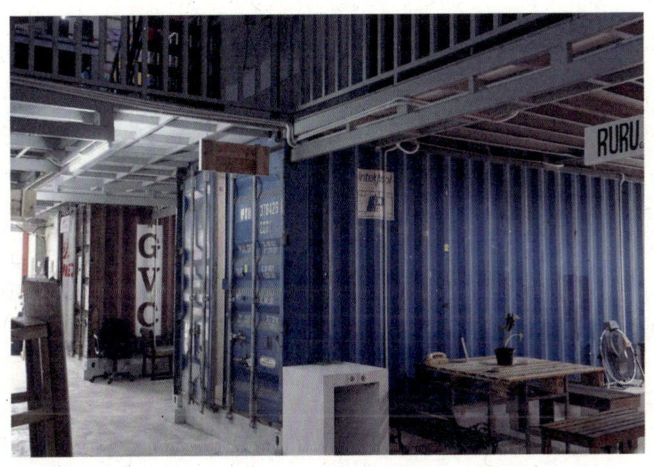
RURU
GVC

PROJECTS

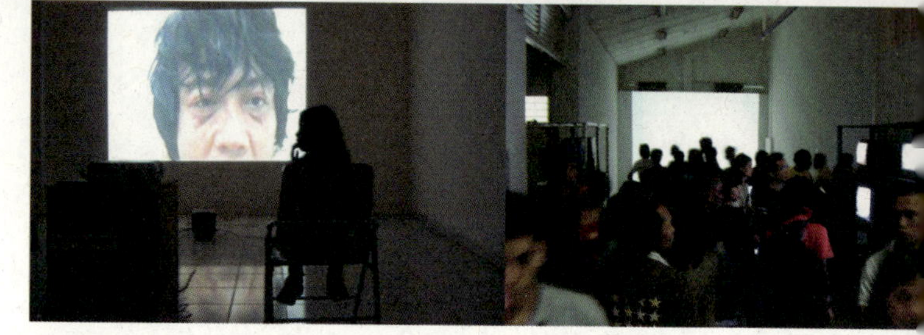

Ok. Video - Jakarta International Video Art Festival

"OUR EXHIBITIONS ARE AN ALIBI."

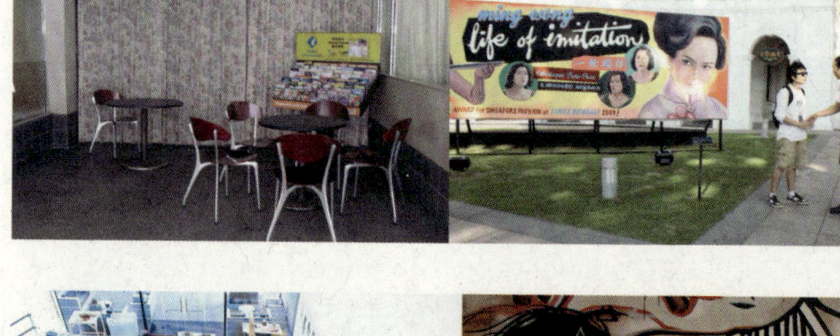

Singapore Night Festival

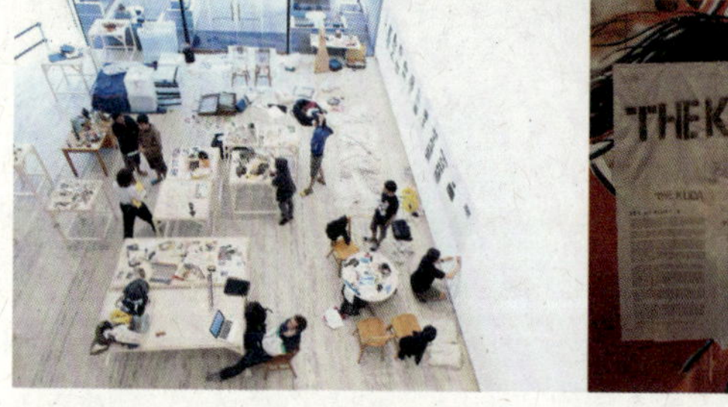

THE KUDA

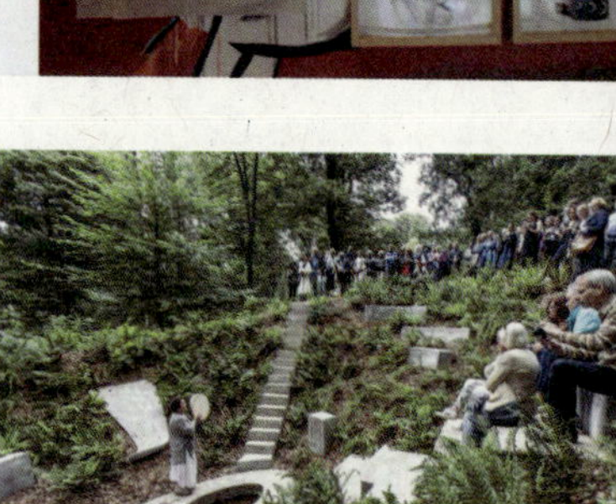

SONSBEEK '16: transACTION

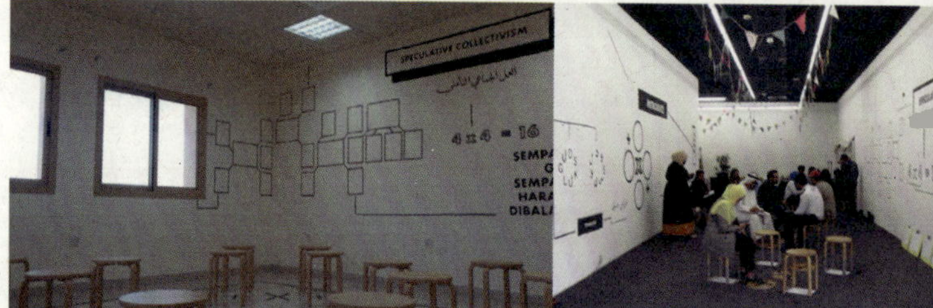

Speculative Collective

p. 158

THE TERM NONGKRONG – INDONESIAN FOR "HANGING OUT TOGETHER" – COULD BE THE OVERARCHING MANTLE FOR THE FOLLOWING PAGES AND OFFER SOME CONTEXT, SINCE THE QUALITY OF RUANGRUPA'S PROJECTS IS ALWAYS A SOCIAL ONE. IN FIVE SHORT INTERVIEWS ON PAST EXHIBITIONS, BIENNIALS, AND FESTIVALS, RUANGRUPA TALKS ABOUT THE STORIES BEHIND THEIR ART ACTIONS SINCE 2003, THE ADVANTAGES FOR THE SURROUNDING NEIGHBORHOODS, AND THEIR IDEA OF MAKING ART BEYOND THE CLASSICAL BIOGRAPHICAL CONFLATIONS OF WORK AND AUTHOR.

p. 162

p. 166

p. 172

p. 180

"TO THIS DAY, ART IN URBAN AND CULTURAL CONTEXTS REMAINS A COMMON THREAD RUNNING THROUGHOUT OUR PRACTICE." CONVERSATION WITH INDRA AMENG

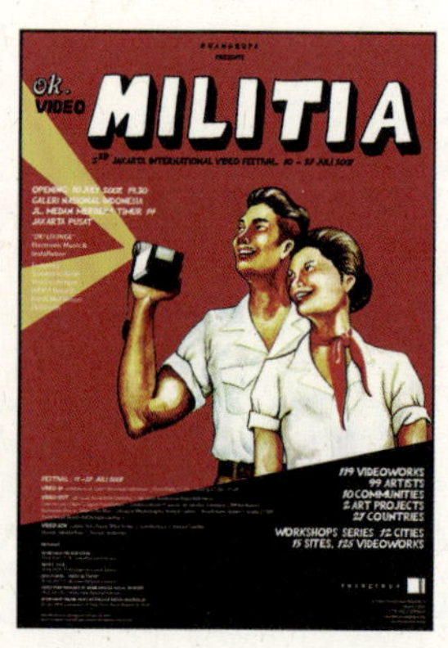

1 about *Ok. Video – Jakarta International Video Art Festival*, at the National Gallery of Indonesia in Jakarta, 2003

TCE You organized the first international video art festival in Indonesia in 2003. Which milieu did the festival emerge in?

IA When we came up with the idea for the *Ok. Video – Jakarta International Video Art Festival,* young artists and students in Indonesia were experimenting with the medium. They were looking for opportunities to make themselves heard in an artistic way using new technologies. We wanted to pick up on these tendencies with the festival and give them a combined platform as well as a laboratory for video art. In the Indonesian art scene, there was neither enough infrastructure nor channels for time-based arts. The galleries and exhibition venues were still heavily focused on object-based art.

TCE Was the video festival intended to oppose television and mass media?

IA Yes, as an alternative to commercial use. The fall of the authoritarian regime in 1998 opened a new chapter in the country's history. Along with all the openings that suddenly emerged, there were also new gaps to be filled. That's why we wanted to find a language that could contribute to socio-cultural debates and cultural discourses. We saw potential for the polyphony we hoped for in video art.

TCE Did you also conceive the video festival with that in mind?

IA Yes, it was to be a place for encounters and discussions. We chose the festival as a format because it allows for a lively exchange as well as more spending time together and learning from each other than an exhibition does.

TCE How did you organize the video festivals?

IA It all started with widespread research in various locations throughout Indonesia, including Java. We also held workshops and residencies with artists from Europe and South America, collected works, set up categories that we transferred to the structure of the video festival, and identified thematic focuses, including identity, politics, mass culture, private and public space, which we used to structure the exhibition within the festival. In addition to experimental video art, there were also music videos and documentary-based films.

TCE What else did the premiere of the video festival include?

IA The first edition included contributions from 56 artists from 19 countries. In addition to the exhibition, we organized artist talks with Krisna Murti (Indonesia), Katsuyuki Hatori (Japan), Greg Streak (South Africa), and Stani Michel (Belgium). There were also workshops and seminars co-organized with Video Art Center Tokyo (Japan) that put video art as an artistic medium up for debate. We asked artist initiatives like PULSE from South Africa, VIDEOTAGE from Hong Kong, and the Video Art Center from Tokyo to organize independent programs within the festival. Based on our research, we also conceived a section for emerging young positions that artistically explored the genre of music videos and represented new developments in the Indonesian art scene.

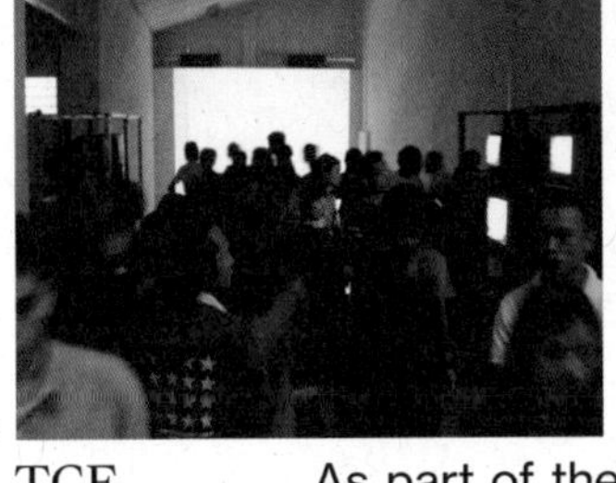

2

TCE As part of the ten-day workshop on *Urban Space in Jakarta*, you collaborated with the German artist Oliver Zwink and the founder of the Bandung Center for New Media Arts, Gustaff H Iskanda. What did you cover there?

IA With the participation of graphic designers, photographers, and filmmakers, we reflected on how urban life can be negotiated within video-based art. To this day, art in urban and cultural contexts remains a common thread running throughout our practice. We're especially interested in having different strategies and approaches to media present at the same time. We developed video works that were connected and shown together at the festival. From the first to the last edition in 2017, we kept interrogating the current state of video art, so the festival's parameters were continually being renegotiated.

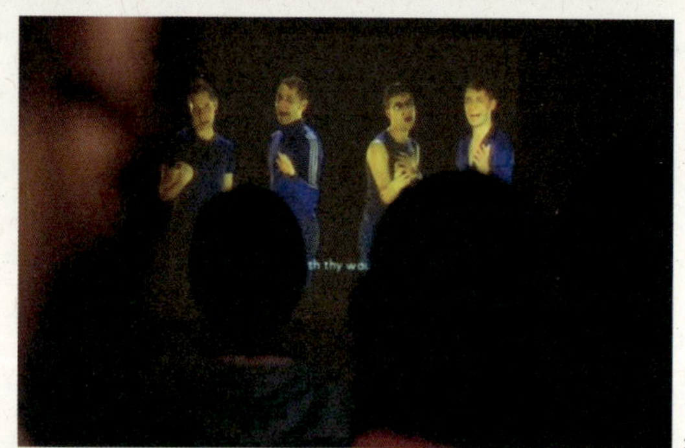
3

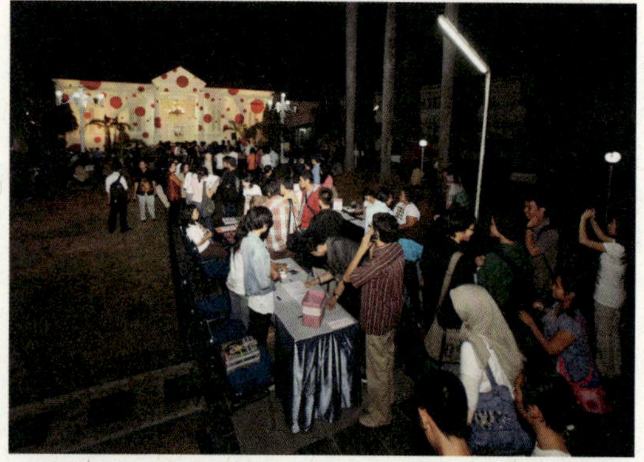
4

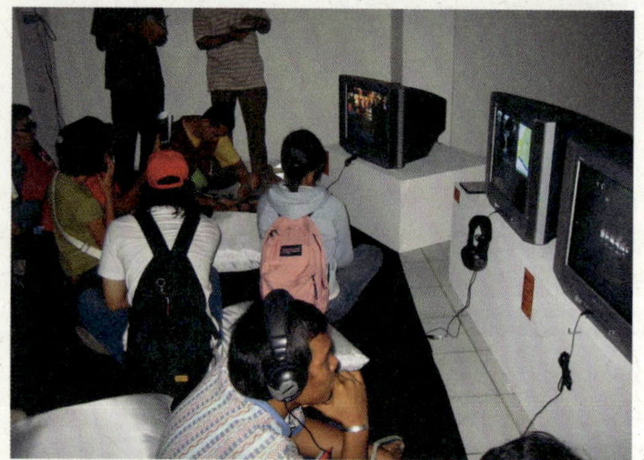
5

Fig. 1: Exhibition poster *Ok. Video – Jakarta International Video Art Festival*, 2003
Fig. 2-7: Impressions of the first *Ok. Video Festival*

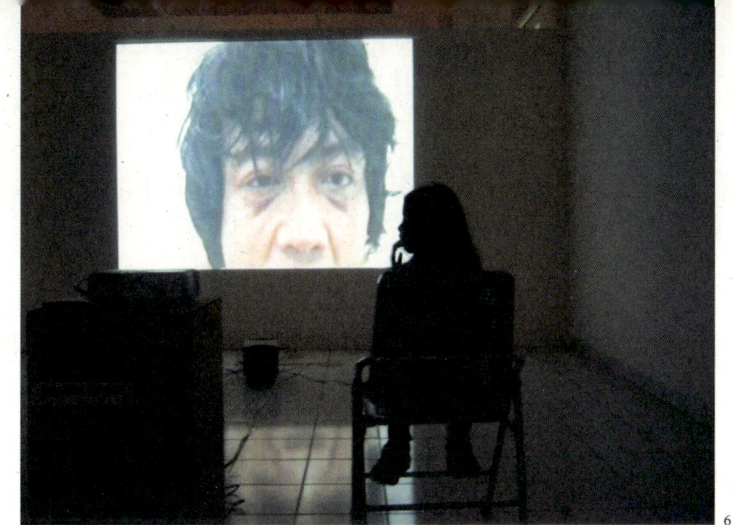
6

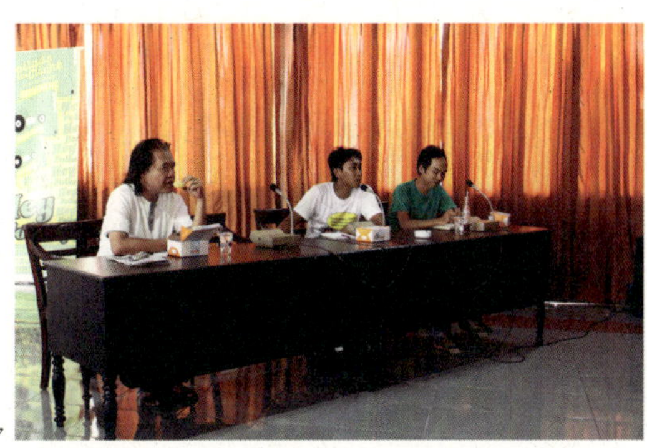
7

“GRAFFITI ILLUSTRATES PEOPLE’S DESIRE TO RENEGOTIATE THE LANDSCAPE IN A VARIETY OF WAYS.” CONVERSATION WITH INDRA AMENG

about the *Singapore Night Festival*, Singapore Art Museum, Singapore, 2010

TCE The transformation of the Singapore Art Museum’s chapel into a music hall involved a lot of people and partners. How did the project come about?

IA We were asking ourselves how we could give the museum a different atmosphere and thought we could create a space for this dynamic by hosting a festival. We weren’t just interested in showing and curating works, but also in creating a framework that went beyond the purely exhibition-based practice of visual art. That’s why we showed video works in the deconsecrated chapel of what is now the museum and also had music performances and workshops take place there. For us, the main priority was combining the atmosphere and excitement of a street festival with a process-oriented curatorial practice. Most of us at ruangrupa play music; some are DJs or play in bands. So it was clear to us from the start that we would invite friends from other bands and also street artists that we liked. The festival, which extended from the museum’s chapel to the street in front of the building, also involved graffiti artists. They created a contemporary aesthetic experience by using graffiti and

1

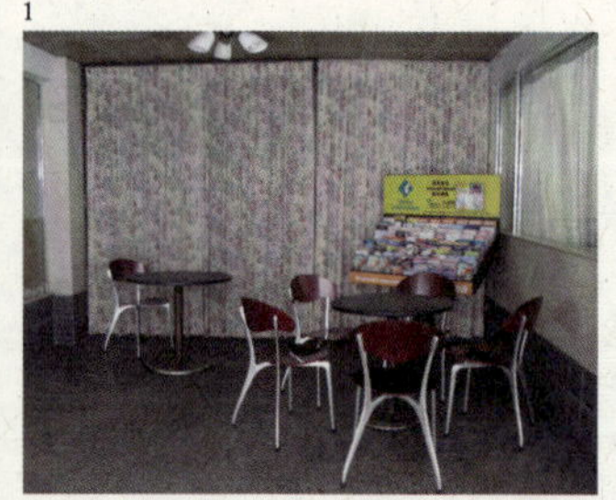

2

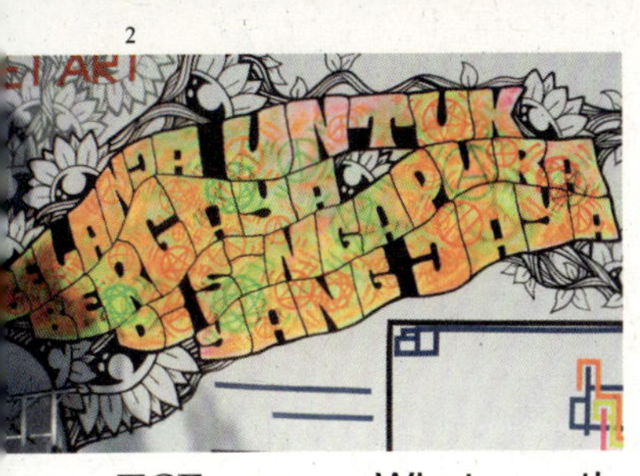

other designs to stimulate a discussion about reactionary artistic works by contemporary artists. And that was the great thing: graffiti illustrated people's desire to renegotiate the landscape in a variety of ways, and it enabled communication between people in urban space on a visual level. Collaborating with street artists is an important part of our ongoing work and research on the development of public space in Jakarta in the past two decades.

TCE What exactly did the program look like?

IA There were workshops on public art, we curated video workshops and special music presentations, and invited other collectives from Jakarta to participate. We also teamed up with the *Jakarta 32°C Student Forum* to involve people from local universities. *Jakarta 32°C* is a dialogue and networking forum for contemporary art and culture, founded by students from all over Jakarta and environs. Initiated by ruangrupa, *Jakarta 32°C* has been collecting ideas and experiments from students since 2004, exploring the latest issues coming out of universities through exhibiting, discussing, and writing.

TCE The themes of the first three editions of the *Ok. Video Festival* in 2005, 2007, and 2009 were comedy, militia, and subversion. What role do these themes play in your daily practice as a collective?

IA The program of the *Ok. Video Festival*, which took place every two years until 2017, had a different theme for each edition: in 2005 it was subversion, in 2007 militia. We explored the idea of how we can understand the camera as a weapon, as a tool to create our own language and identity, both for the future and when looking back at history. Comedy was the theme in 2009 and an opportunity to practice criticism through a different kind of language, the kind of criticism that one might not otherwise be able to formulate in public due to restrictions and censorship. The *Singapore Night Festival* in 2010 thus presented a best-of from these previous editions of the *Ok. Video Festival* in Jakarta.

TCE What role did karaoke play in the project?

IA (laughs) Our hearts are always open for karaoke – it's also a fun part of many of our openings or when we host parties in our art space. One of our colleagues in ruangrupa, oomleo, developed a machine that allows you to create midi arrangements from any kind of music or song. People always love it, and that's another reason why karaoke is a consistent element in many of our projects and exhibitions.

TCE Where will karaoke take place in Kassel?

IA We will arrange a series of karaoke parties, one of them will take place at the Friedrichsplatz.

ming wong
life of imitation
一世模仿
Kehidupan Pura-Pura
உண்மையற்ற வாழ்க்கை
VARD for SINGAPORE PAVILION at VENICE BIENNALE 2009!

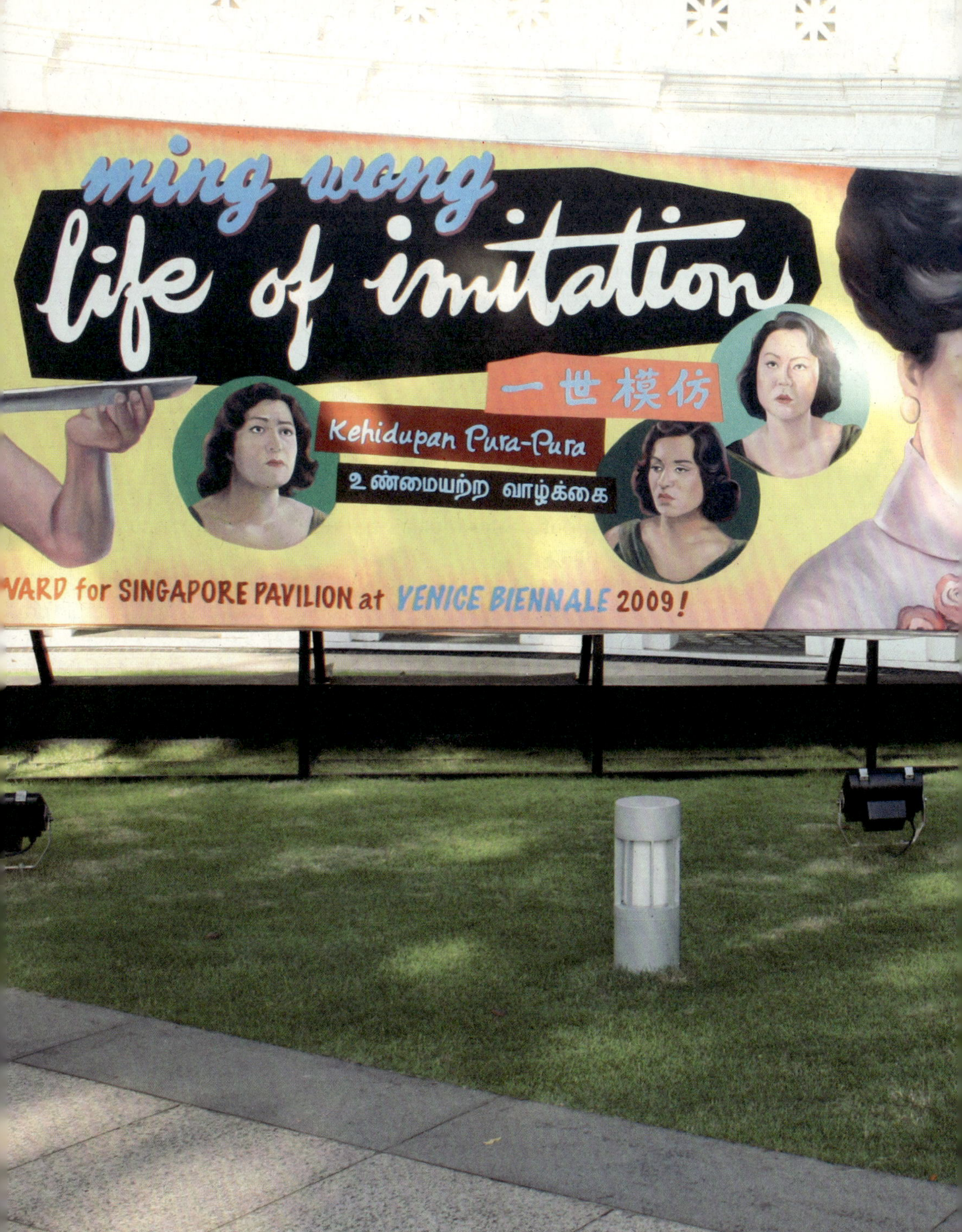

3

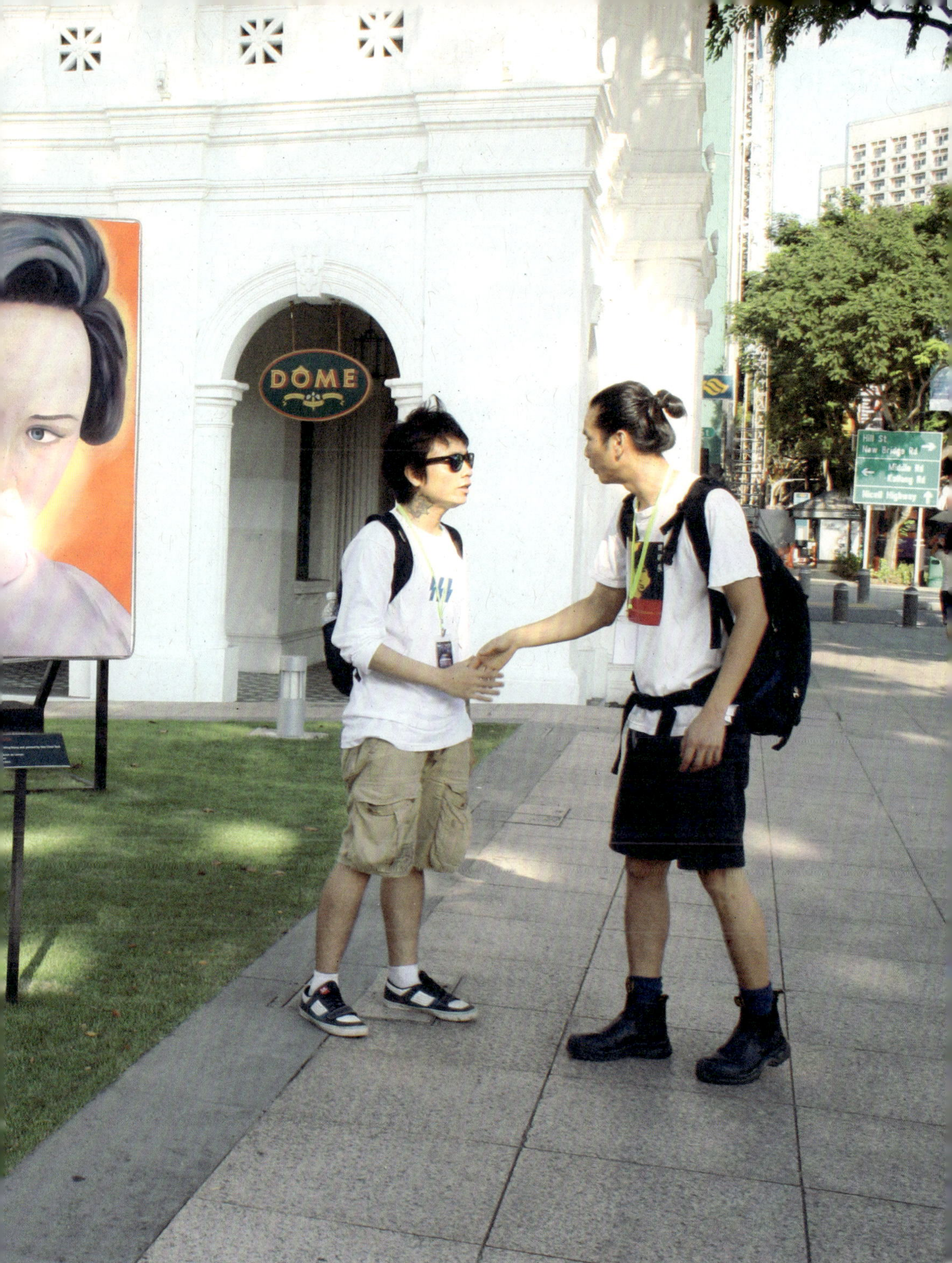

Fig. 1: *Singapore Night Festival*, 2010
Fig. 2: Street art was an elementary component of the *Singapore Night Festival*
Fig. 3: Installation in front of the Singapore Art Museum during the *Singapore Night Festival*

"WE WANTED TO WRITE OUR OWN HISTORY OF PUNK IN THE 1970S." CONVERSATION WITH INDRA AMENG

about *THE KUDA: The Untold Story of Indonesian Underground Music in the 70s*, 7th Asia Pacific Triennial of Contemporary Art (APT7), Brisbane, 2012

TCE The exhibition functioned as a mini-museum of memorabilia related to the story of a fictional Indonesian band and its influence on Brisbane's music scene. How did the project come about?

IA Brisbane has a distinct underground music scene. When we got invited to participate in the Asia Pacific Triennial, it quickly became clear to us that we would focus on this topic. During our first research trip to Brisbane, we met people from the city's music scene and local community radio stations. We found out there was a great story behind it that we could link to our own experiences. We were primarily interested in the history of punk music in Brisbane during the 70s. In the 70s and much of the 80s, Queensland was a police state under Joh Bjelke-Petersen, the longest-serving premier to date. Many remember him primarily for his rigid control of all areas of government and his anti-democratic attitude toward public protest. There are major parallels to what we had to experience under Suharto's regime. It was a time marked by censorship and seething student movements that were banned from any political activity due to a law that was newly implemented in Indonesia at the time.
Many young people at the time thus felt the need to express their ideas and make themselves heard through art and, of course, music. At that time, punk music wasn't established as a genre yet, since mostly hard rock was being played. Punk was a purely underground sound and

1

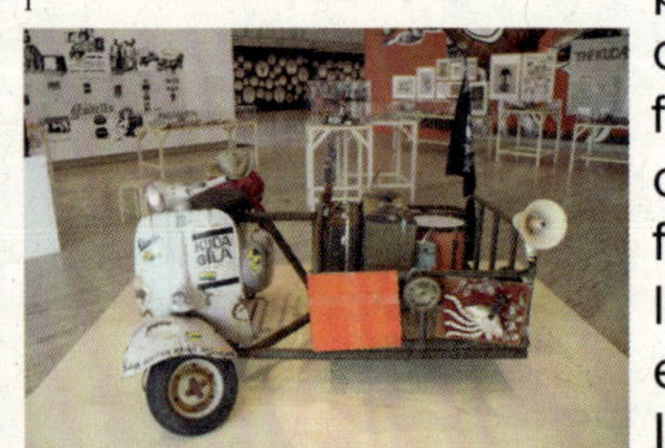

happened in hiding. There were similar subcultural codes and scenes in Brisbane. So we made a mockumentary about a young group of Indonesian students who start a punk band. In the fictional documentary, they record their first demo tape, which coincidentally ends up in Brisbane and gets broadcast there, bringing them fame. That was the narrative framework, and working through it culminated in an installation at the Triennial, accompanied by a historical timeline of events at the time.

TCE How did you conceive the exhibition and organize the production? What did the process look like?

IA Since we work collectively, we always try to work on something related to our daily lives and situations in Indonesia. With *THE KUDA* project, we wanted to write our own history of punk in the 70s. By telling our own version of the story, we were able to find new narratives – even offer completely different ones – and play with the history, make it our own. In terms of the

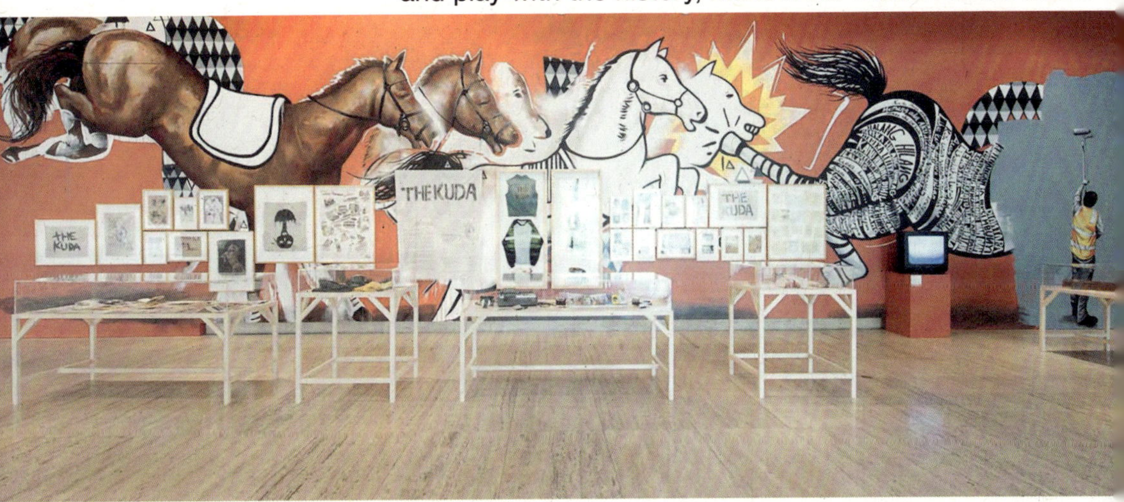

2

process, we didn't just work on the project as ruangrupa, but as is often the case, we found other partners within the thematic field. For *KUDA*, we worked with musicians, other researchers, and historians to develop the installation. We also drew heavily on interviews with student activists from the period, as well as with politicians and friends in Brisbane. The musicans, that acted the band members of *THE KUDA*, are actually ina a real band themselves. Together we recorded a new song for this specific project. In addition to the film and the history timeline, the project included sound and memorabilia from the band: display cases with items belonging to the band, such as a notebook, photos, a costume, musical instruments, and a collection of old newspapers and magazines from the 70s.

TCE What role does music play for ruangrupa?

IA We all have musical backgrounds. I myself work as a producer and manage a band. This is related to the fact that we organized music festivals as students in the 90s. Of course, we were also protesting through this music. Anyone organizing a concert back then knew it was subversive.

TCE What role does music play in Indonesian culture?

IA Music is deeply rooted in Indonesian culture. We use music in many rituals and gatherings. As a country with over 300 ethnic groups, there are about 718 regional languages throughout the Indonesian archipelago. Those languages also have different dialects and tonalities. This creates a stunningly diverse array of sounds and musical landscapes. So music helps us Indonesians to understand each other in a way that goes beyond the differences between languages, dialects, and ways of expression. Music is the glue to build kinship in Indonesian society.

3

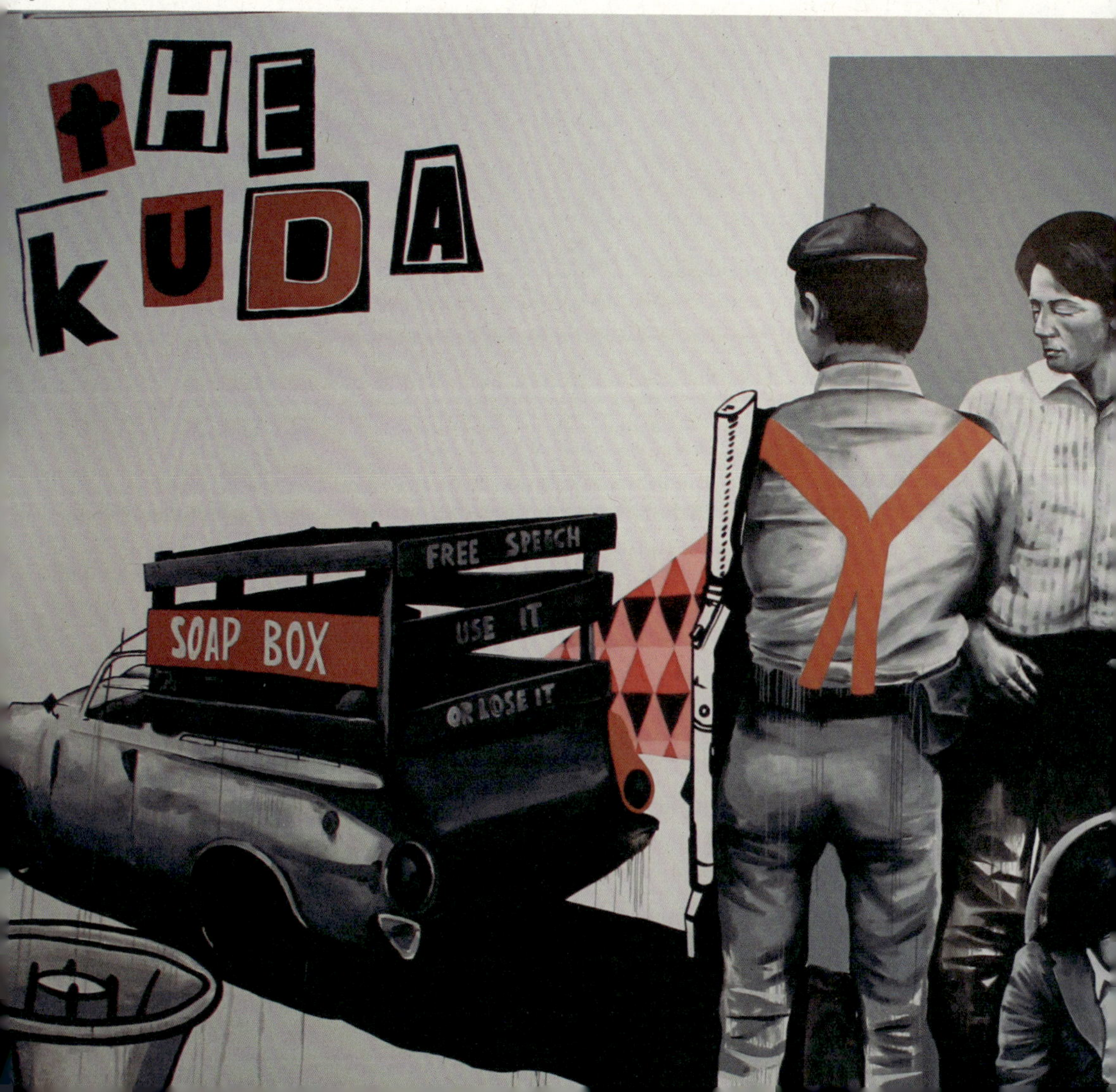

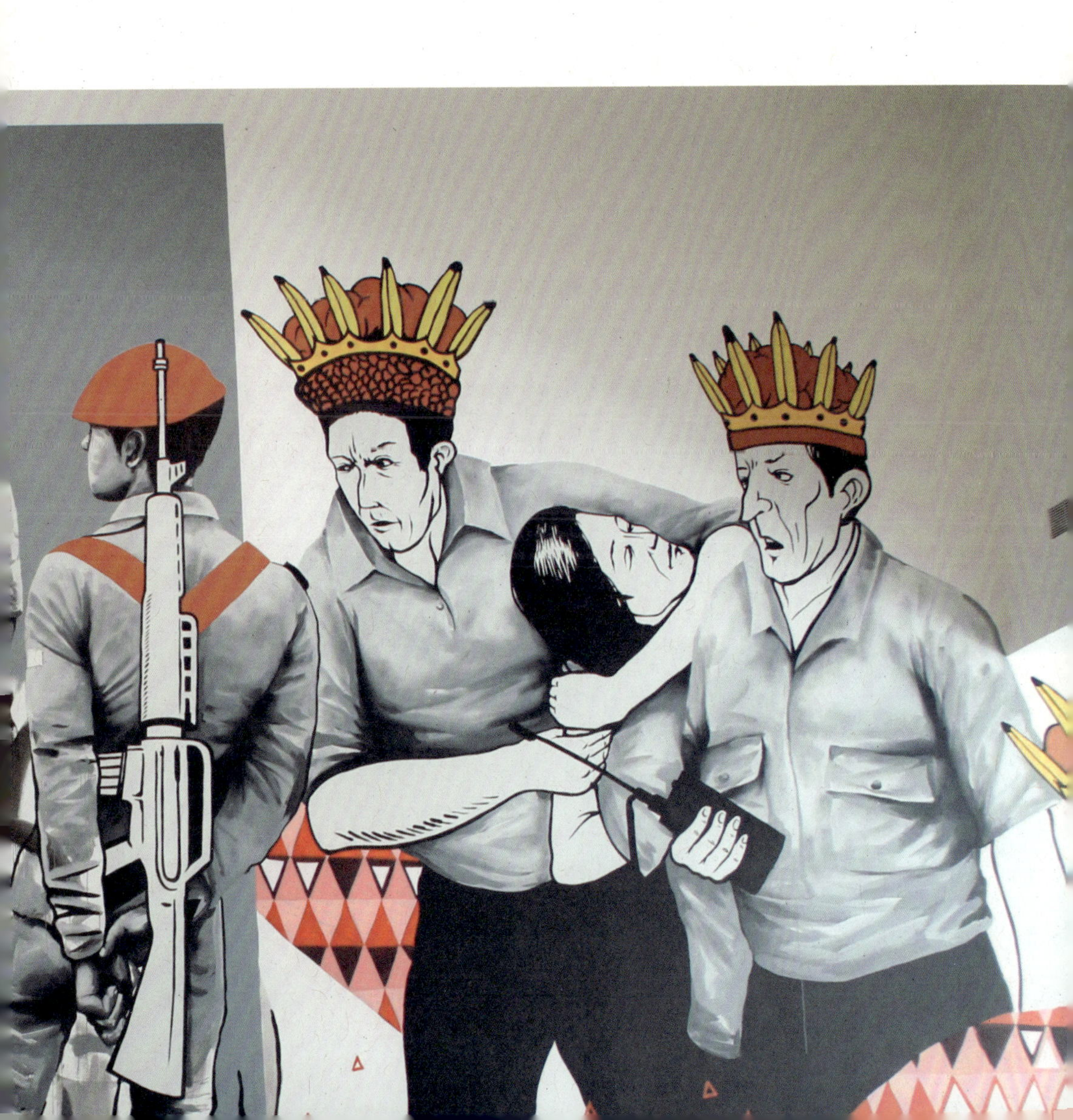

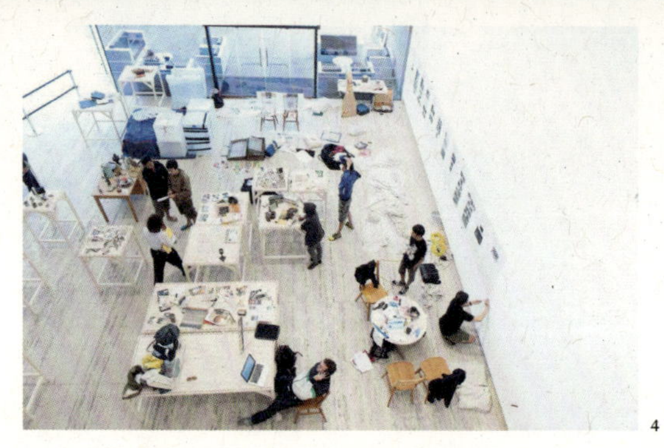

4

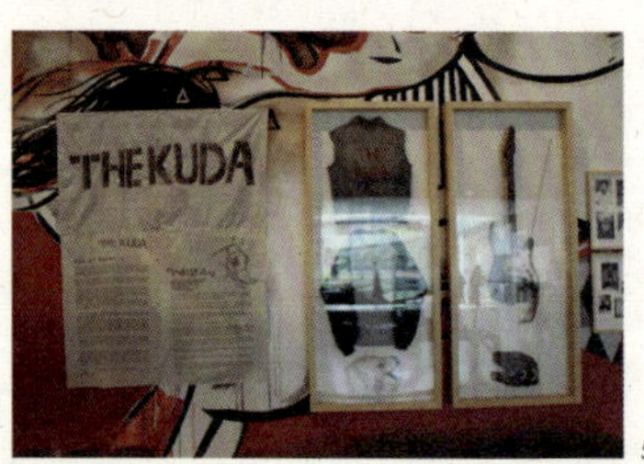

5

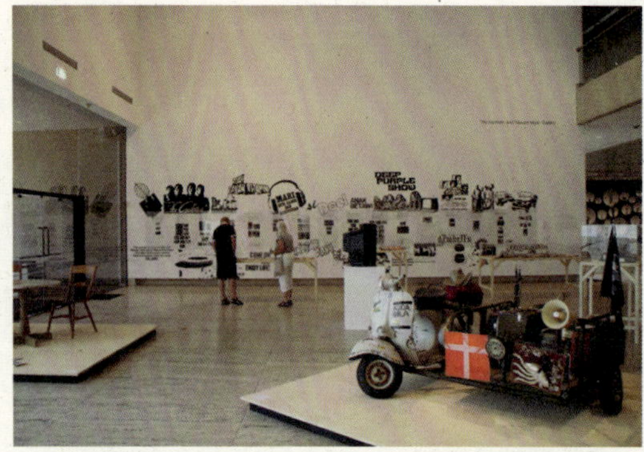

6

Fig. 1–10: Installation view *THE KUDA*, 2012

father
MARI
KITA HADIR
DAN
SUKSESKAN
si Doel
ANAK
COME ON
AND
DIKEJAR
DOSA
7

THE KUDA
8

9

JANCUK
10

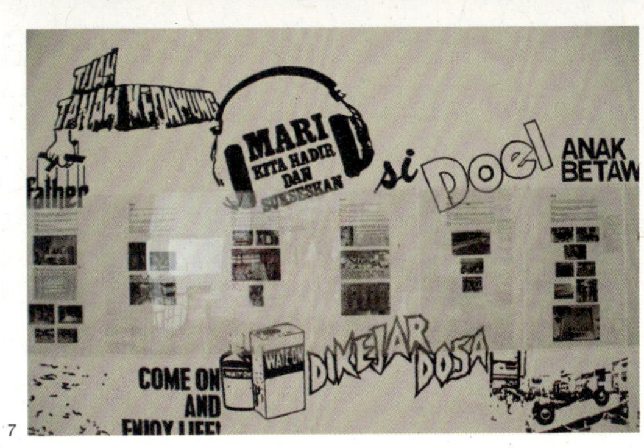

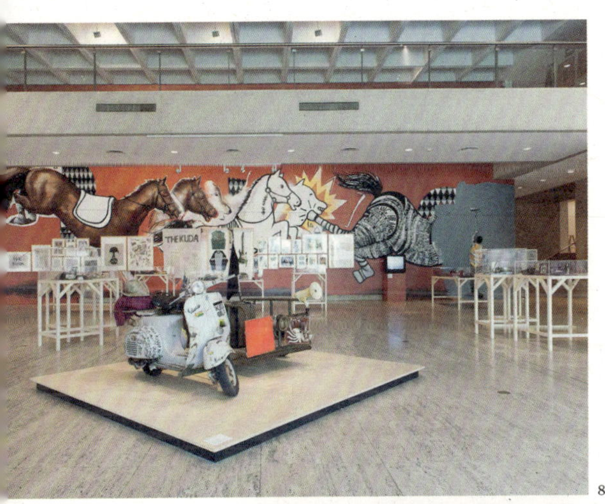

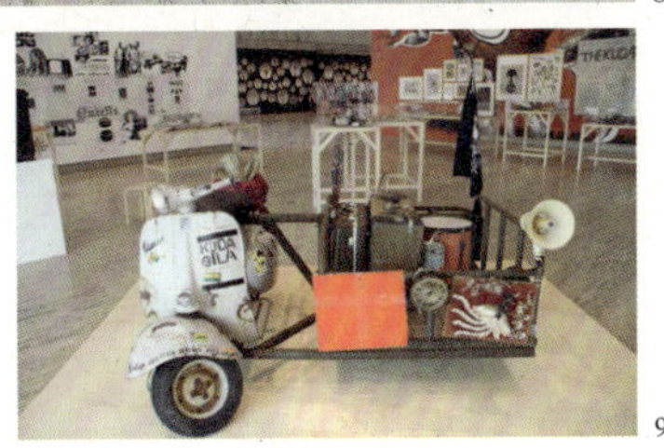

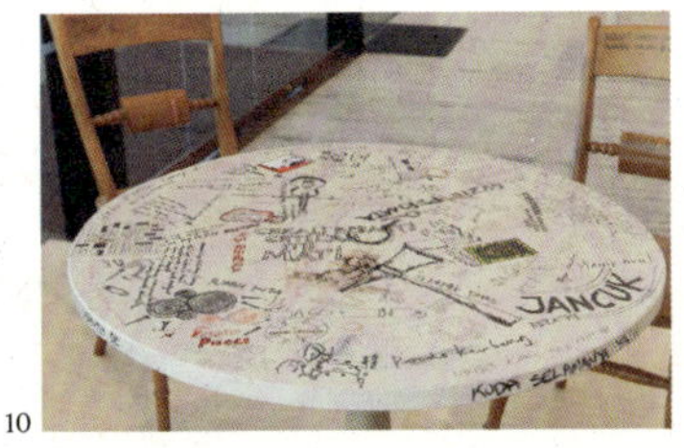

"SONSBEEK WAS THE FIRST TIME RUANGRUPA CURATED OUTSIDE OF INDONESIA." INTERVIEW WITH FARID RAKUN

about *SONSBEEK '16: transACTION*, Park Sonsbeek, Museum Arnhem, Arnhem, 2016

TCE When researching *SONSBEEK '16*, you immediately notice that it was about bringing people together and connecting them with and through art. ruangrupa presented a variety of media: from sculptures, installations, performances, and parades through the city, to music, food, talks, and simply inviting people to hang out together. Were you trying out a different approach than you would usually use for this special occasion?

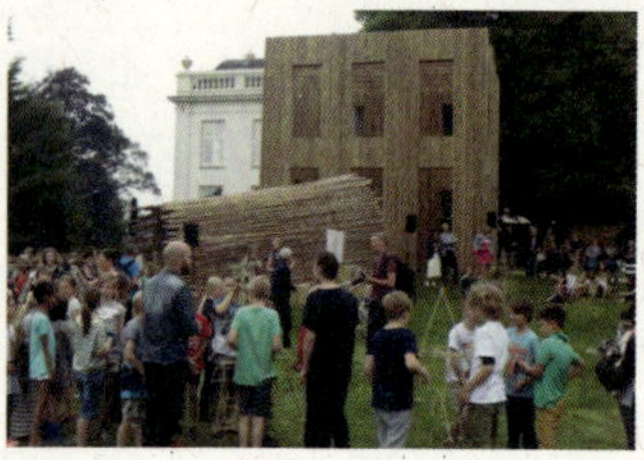

1

FR *SONSBEEK* was the first time ruangrupa curated something as a group outside of Indonesia. Some of us had done it before as individuals, but it was new for us as a group. At the same time, *SONSBEEK* was just being revived. Until then, the exhibition, which was conceived as a biennial, had only been held at irregular intervals every five, eight, or even ten years. 2016 was the first time that the organizers planned for it to happen every four years. The selection process was also interesting. All the shortlisted curators met in Arnhem to visit the city. So we knew who else was applying for the curator position, which is quite different from documenta, for example. So there were a lot of first times at *SONSBEEK*.

TCE How did all these first times influence your work for *SONSBEEK* or beyond?

FR We learned a lot. For example, how to curate when you have to. None of us were trained as curators. Of course we curated our own events and all sorts of things in different formats. But we were self-taught, since there wasn't any training for curators in Indonesia back then. So we're very aware of the fact that when we say we're curating or doing events in our own way, it might not necessarily correspond with what the formal system or a school would call curating.

TCE In curating, it's also crucial to find your own way. People should be braver, I think.

FR We do it out of necessity, not because of a political stance or for the sake of positioning. It's the result of our situation. And like you said, we're used to mixing a lot of things together. For *SONSBEEK*, we asked our friends to join at some point. There were some new ones among them, but most we already knew. It's a very different approach than the one we're using now for documenta. *SONSBEEK* taught us that it makes sense to meet friends more regularly and work with local artists. Certain things that we're now doing at documenta fifteen were already presented at *SONSBEEK*. The idea of the house as an exhibition is important. In Dutch we called it *ruru huis*, in German it's now called *ruruHaus*. In *SONSBEEK* the main course, so to speak, was the public park. It was the part of the exhibition that we wanted to encourage the artists to create works for, that wouldn't just be seen, but also experienced as space. It allowed the audience to connect to the work and empathize with it.

TCE You also used the Museum Arnhem and collaborated with the local university. Was this something that had been done before, or did you initiate it?

FR *SONSBEEK* and the museum had already agreed to collaborate. We used this opportunity to show works that function differently than the ones for public spaces. It was a nice experience because we'd never done anything like that before.

TCE Another first. You chose the theme *transACTION* for *SONSBEEK*. In this context, ruangrupa specifically mentioned the idea of exchange and storytelling.

FR In retrospect, the transaction happened for us because we learned from the experience. One example: instead of developing a new concept for documenta, we invited it to participate in our journey. We learned that from *SONSBEEK*, where we did the exact opposite. Now, we first try to distill what we've done and turn it into seeds, which is basically what we mean by transaction. Ultimately, we didn't do anything just for the sake of *SONSBEEK*; rather it contributed to our lives, our work in Jakarta, and now documenta fifteen. As for the exhibition, the works themselves talked about exchange, for example, about a rainforest and carbon trading. Others were about cultural transactions through legal and illegal immigration, or the exchange of playgrounds between Jakarta and Amsterdam. The list goes on. Other aspects were the *transACTION* of knowledge, storytelling with the museum, a kind of *transHISTORY*, as well as the

2

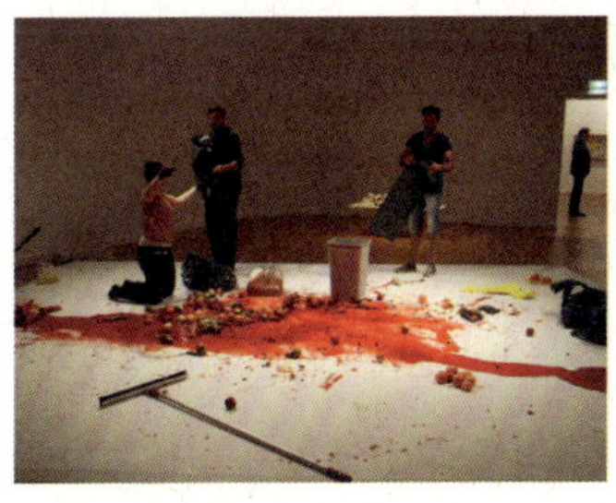

implementation of the *transACTION* with local artists, too.

TCE How did you integrate storytelling into *SONSBEEK*. Was it more of an underlying idea that flowed into everything, or did you also address it specifically?

FR We've expanded the storytelling a bit more and insist on it at documenta as well. While producing *SONSBEEK*, we realized that we lacked a deep idea of storytelling. It was difficult for us to communicate what we were doing before the exhibition, what our values were, what the theme was, etc. We understood that storytelling, seen cosmologically, is part of the experience and that it helps communicate our values. Some works, in turn, included storytelling, especially those in the museum. Most of them contained a narrative element, even if it wasn't necessarily linear. Another aspect is that many of the people we work with haven't been theorized yet. So it's often hard for them and us to argue that they're coming from a certain place in terms of content and thought, one that is just as valuable as those that have already been theorized or occupy a recognized position within existing knowledge. A lot of the values we start from – hanging out together, the way we understand sufficiency and talk about sustainability in our practice or economics – come from a place of "not knowing." Storytelling is helpful here. It broadens your perspective. Rather than being tied down to a particular understanding, stories allow different perspectives to be shared.

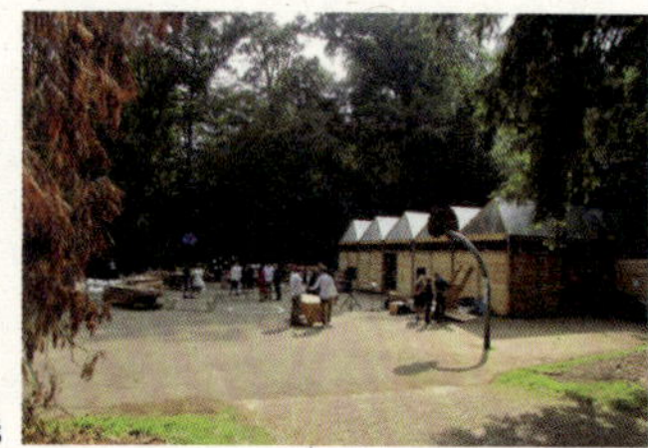
3

TCE I understand that *SONSBEEK* was such an important stop for you and it led you to where you are now. Looking back, what aspect stands out the most for you?

FR To be honest: a rather traumatic one, namely that we forgot Jakarta for a while. This also made us aware of certain limits to our sensibility. We also had to rethink the connection between Indonesia and the Netherlands, and ask ourselves how we deal with it today. Having to rethink these kinds of things wasn't always a blessing. One thing we're continuing is the concept of the house. We think of the *ruru house* as a kind of space or particular strategy for creating something. We first used the term in *SONSBEEK* in dutch which is ruru huis. It was also the first time that we deliberately used it as a curatorial strategy. By now we know that we always need a space for a *ruru house* in each new context; it's non-negotiable. That said, we stick to the idea of not coming up with a theme or specific new idea for something that we need to realize somewhere else, especially in Western Europe. To get back to your question about storytelling: we tried using a different kind of language. Not every artist liked it: we asked people who don't come from the art world, and thus don't use art language, to write about the works for our catalogue action book. To this day, we're still trying to overcome these language barriers. We certainly aren't the only ones who think art jargon is very alienating to outsiders.

TCE Going back to the idea of curating, what have you learned for yourselves in terms of curating? I mean, sometimes it's almost an insult to even use that word. Everyone wants to be a curator.

FR We don't want to be curators because of the associated power relations and huge responsibility. Sometimes when people who curate or do curatorial programs talk to us, we realize that we see things differently, that calling what we do curating might also be an insult to them as well. We learn a lot from what they do, but there are a lot of people who can do it better than us. We know we shouldn't be curators, but it's an extension of what we do, and we know how important these kinds of events are for the people and the ideas, and also simply for the people we can bring together. We always know more as a result, so we want to share documenta as a resource bank with a lot of people, as many people as possible.

4

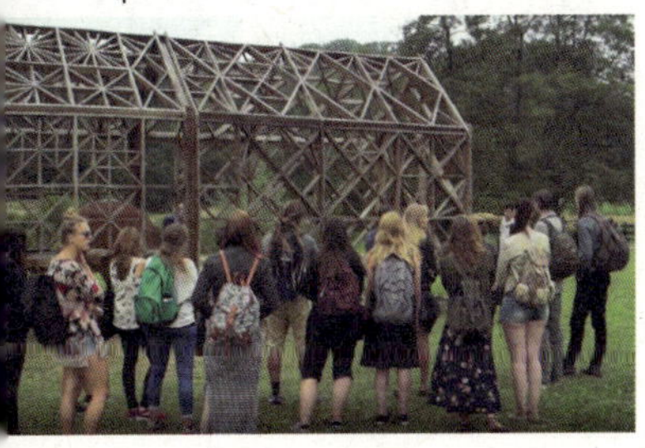

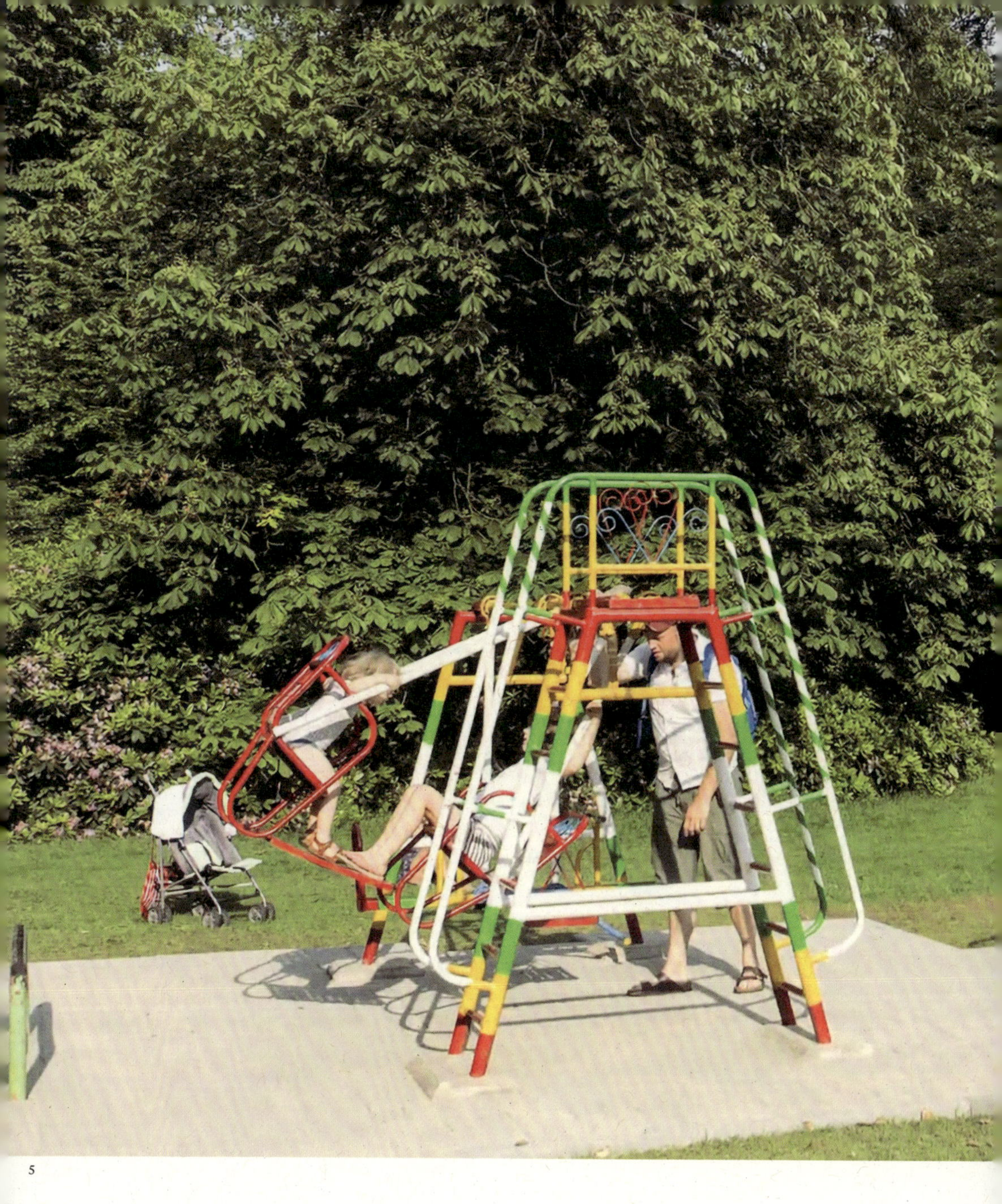

5

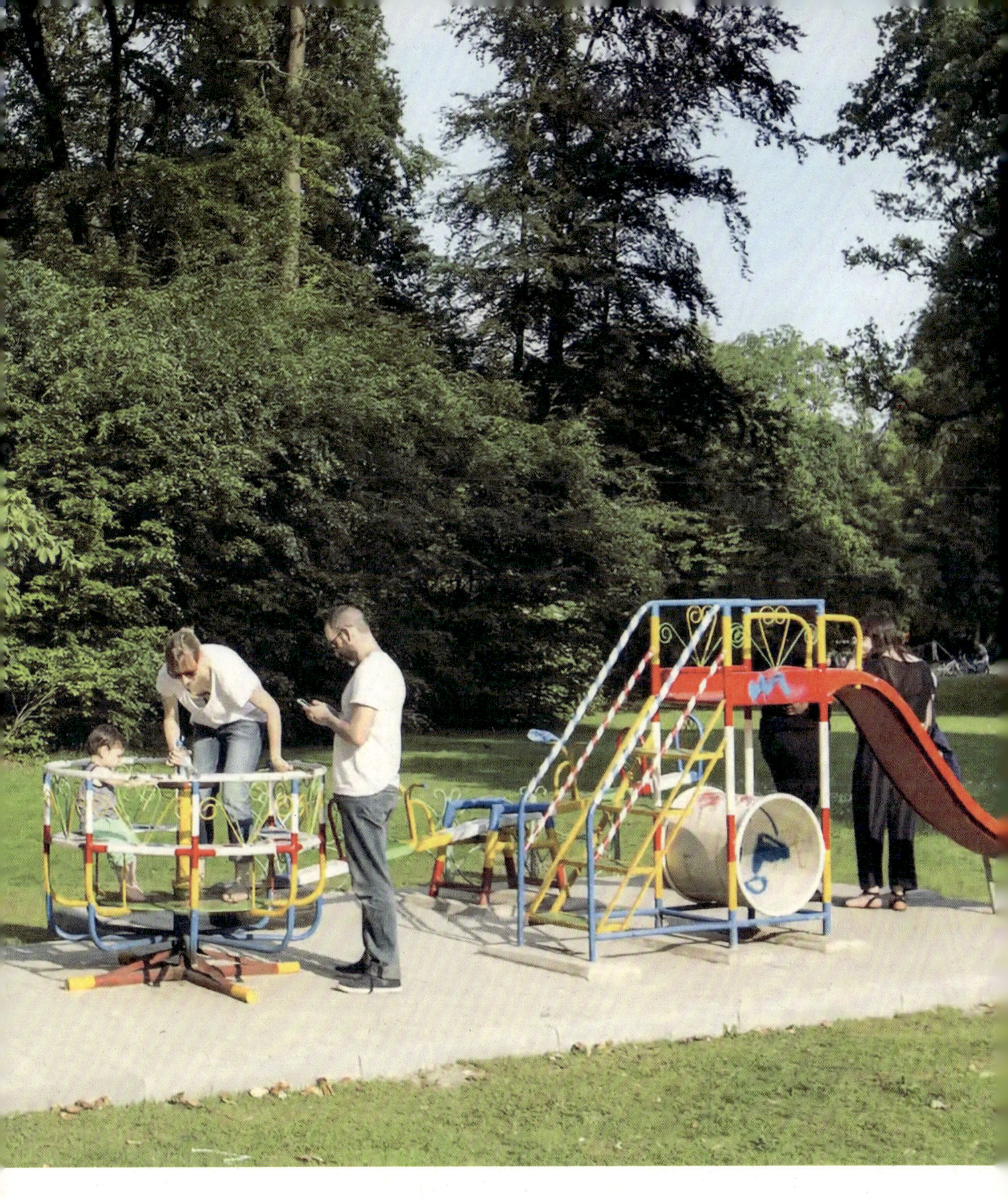

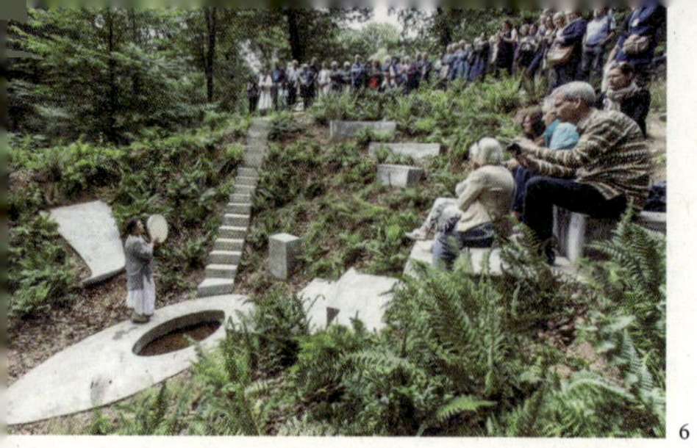
6

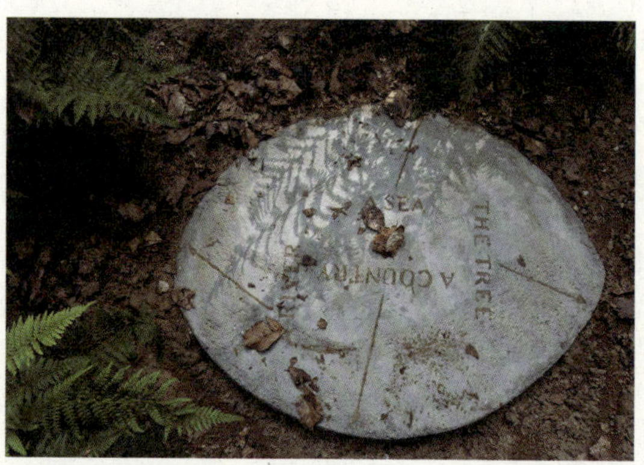

7

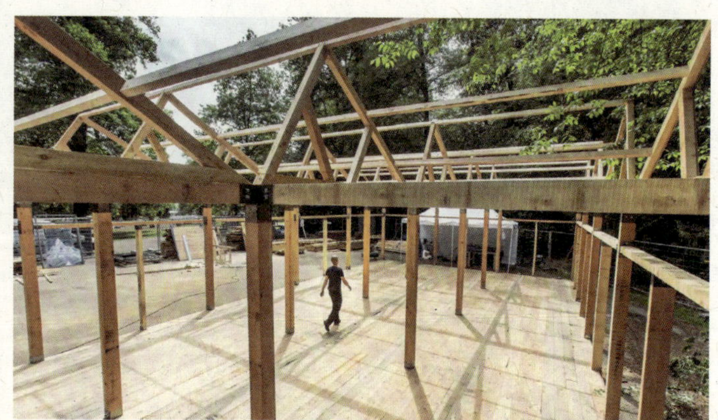
8

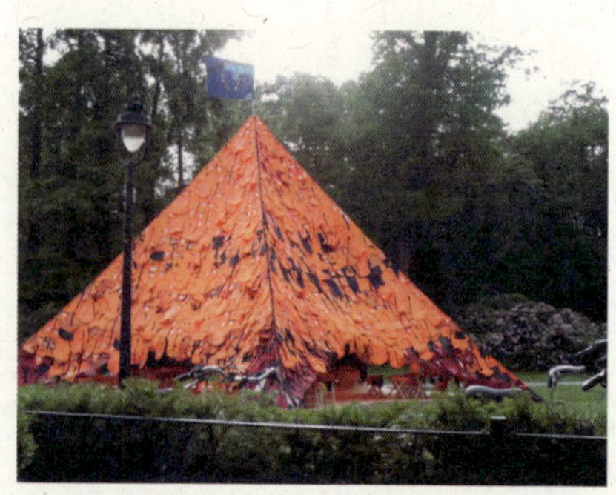
9

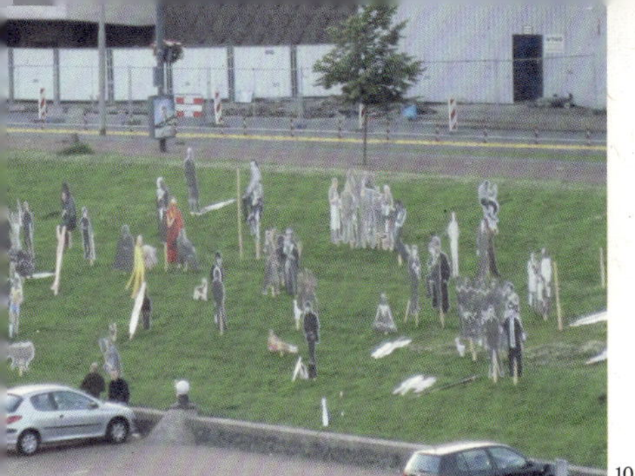
10

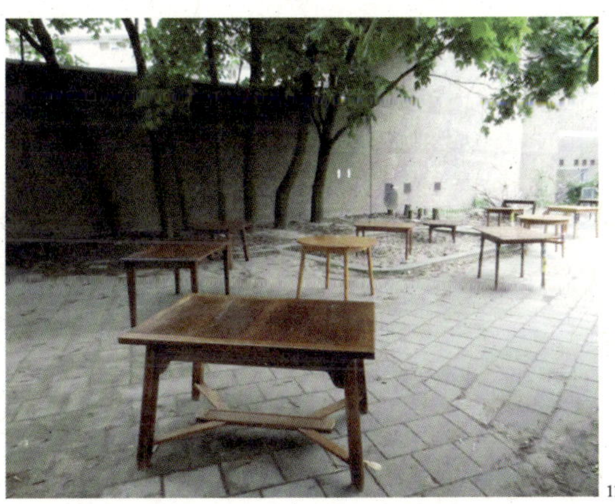
11

Fig. 1-2: Impressions from *SONSBEEK '16*
Fig. 3: Wedding party during *SONSBEEK '16*
Fig. 5-11: Impressions *SONSBEEK '16*

"B-MOVIE ABOUT A BILINGUAL SHOE STORE" INTERVIEW WITH FARID RAKUN

about *Speculative Collective*, Sharjah Biennale 14, Sharjah, 2019

TCE You developed the project *Speculative Collective* for the Sharjah Biennial 14 in 2019. What was it about?

FR It was part of the exhibition *Leaving the Echo Chamber* curated by Zoe Butt. We decided to host the project as *Gudskul*. It was one of the first attempts to formulate an independent expression for our coalition with Grafis Huru Hara and Serrum. It's something we keep testing out and rebalancing to this day. When we arrived, we found out that the Sharjah Art Foundation, which hosts the Sharjah Biennial, has an education department. So there was already a sustainable structure that we could dock our contribution into. In addition to the participatory setting we designed for the exhibition at the Collections Building in Arts Square, we organized additional workshops and traveled to locations outside the city such as the Al Madam Art Centre and the Khorfakkan Art Centre, in the central and eastern regions of the Emirates. With *Speculative Collective*, we wanted to initiate an exercise in collective practice. It began with an existing structure, the *Knowledge Market* – an experimental module that was originally conceived by Serrum but has gradually merged with *Gudskul's* collective practice over time. We designed a setting for it with graphic elements, wall texts, and an arrangement of chairs to facilitate the module's use.

Ideally, strangers would meet each other there to share knowledge from their own stockpile in a brief, one-hour session. This was done by alternately slipping into the roles of teacher and student. In the context of the *Knowledge Market*, we chose the term *Knowledge Sharing* for this kind of exchange. Since we didn't think that two individuals coming together counted as a collective yet, our next step was to bring about the formation of larger groups, and we expanded the practice of the *Knowledge Market*.

TCE What did this expansion look like?

FR We developed two additional phases of coming together that tied into *Knowledge Sharing*: *Introduce Your Friend* and *Speculative Collectivism*. The *Knowledge Sharing* pairs that formed

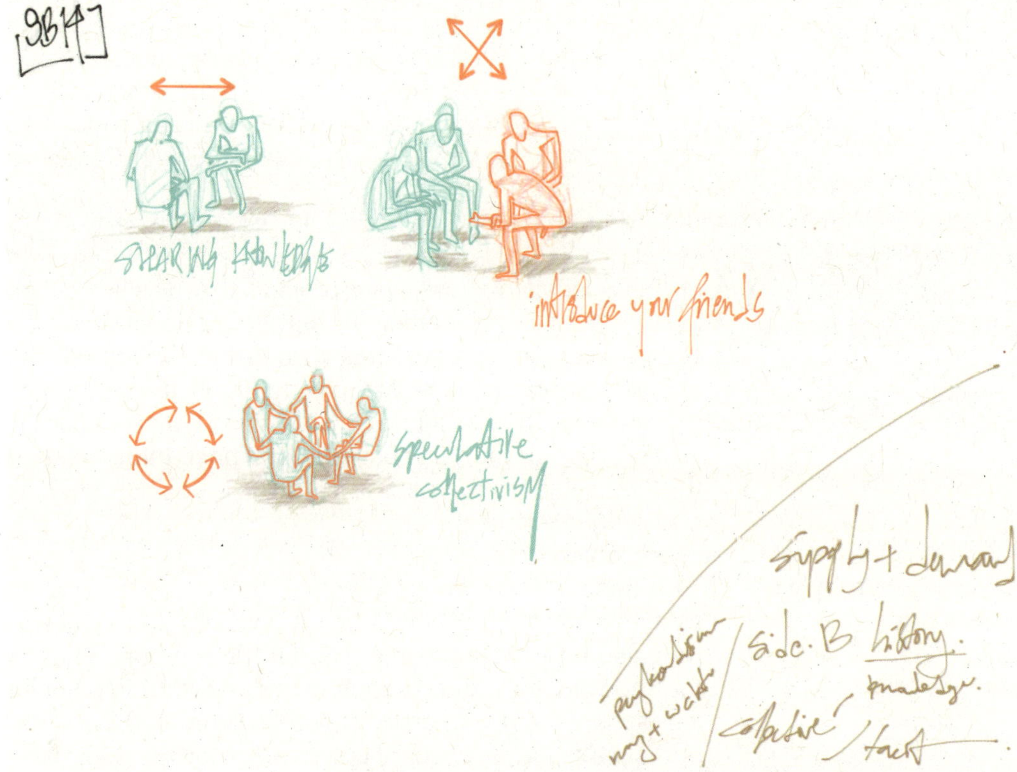

1 had the option of joining up with another duo that had also just been formed. Within this constellation, the participants introduced each other (*Introduce Your Friend*) and exchanged their acquired knowledge after the group of four has been formed. This then served as the basis for speculating together about what kind of collective could be formed, what to call it, and what sustainable project could be created based on the group's shared knowledge resources *(Speculative Collectivism)*. The participants' exchanges would be transferred into speculations about a fictional collective.

TCE How should we imagine this form of exchange and speculation?

FR Suppose the first duo were to teach each other a few German and Indonesian lines, and the other pair were to exchange ideas about a certain way of tying shoes and flying kites, the third phase of *Speculative Collectivism* could result in a collective fantasy about a bilingual shoe store that offered kite-flying workshops.

TCE Which exchanges on site do you remember most?

FR The dialogue between people from different milieus and professions, as well as the subsequent clash between different forms of knowledge. Among the participants there was a maintenance man who shared tricks and instructions for nifty maneuvers in everyday life. He shared tips on the fastest way to clean a large floor, how to survive in a city like Sharjah, where to find the cheapest places to eat. On the other hand, we had participants in leadership positions at large institutions who spoke about how to win over sponsors.

TCE Tooling plays an important role in your work. What does this term mean for you, and what role does it play in the *Speculative Collective* in particular?

FR We understand Tooling as a kind of *Sharing Advice* and hope that others can take something from the process we've initiated. In the *Speculative Collective* project, this was specifically expressed in the setting we devised. The site-specific settings served as a tool that guided the process of the *Knowledge Market*. The participants had the opportunity to document their exchanges. Something we now call Harvesting, though we didn't use the term back then. We then used these collective records to design a zine published as part of the biennial.

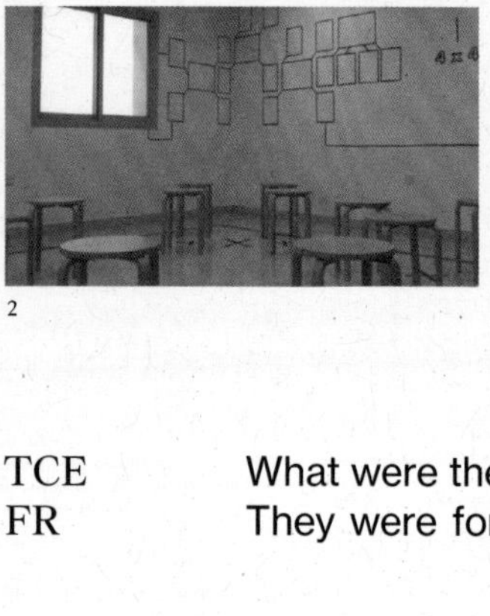

2

TCE What were the certificates for?

FR They were for the people who wanted to stay in touch and functioned as a manifestation of what they had worked on together. It was also a kind of agreement about the symbolic value of the knowledge they had acquired together that functioned independently of economic rationales. Prompted by us, the participants made a pact of collective co-ownership of this knowledge. An official document becomes something else when four people are involved. This creates a conversation about how collective ownership works: Who signs the certificate? Who gets to keep it? Or should ownership rotate among themselves?

TCE Did this elicit a broader conversation about authorship and ownership?

FR Yes, the certificate became a generator for conversations about these issues. The idea of collective ownership had to be negotiated, and the project offered a model situation for that. Otherwise they could have just torn the certificate into four pieces. We don't have the answers either, but we're curious to see how conversations like this unfold.

TCE Let's go back to the importance of knowledge and how that fed into the *Speculative Collective* project.

FR It was important to us that participants playfully experience how anyone can take on the roles of student and teacher, that forming a collective doesn't have to be complicated, and that these things primarily depend on our willingness. Moreover, we're interested in what knowledge is created and what value we give it when we act collectively. The education imparted by most schools is based on the notion of singular uniqueness: we're taught to define our own value in terms of marketability. In the collective, we learn that it isn't about surpassing ourselves or others.

TCE Your concept of *B-knowledge*, which you derived from the idea of B-movies, probably ties into this thought process.

FR That's the concept we were working with at the time. We love B-movies as a concept and a figure of thought. This descriptive category opens up a space for alternative ways of evaluating knowledge. We conceive of *B-knowledge* as a kind of knowledge that's deemed personally valuable, but lies outside the sphere of what is regularly measured in terms of value. Our application of *B-knowledge* allowed a framework for articulating such forms of knowledge to emerge. With the project in Sharjah, we wanted to give an impression of our *Gudskul* practice.

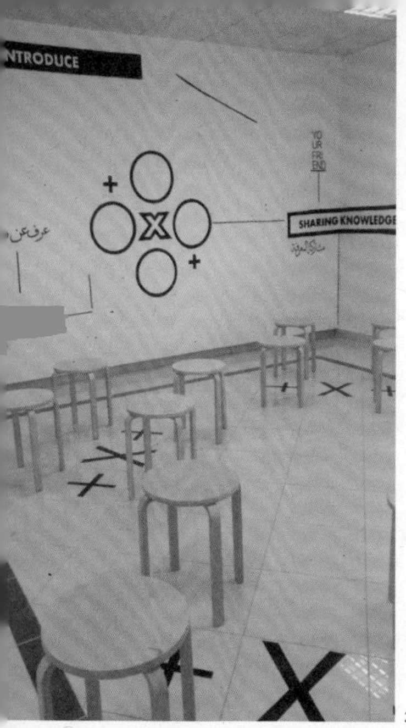

3

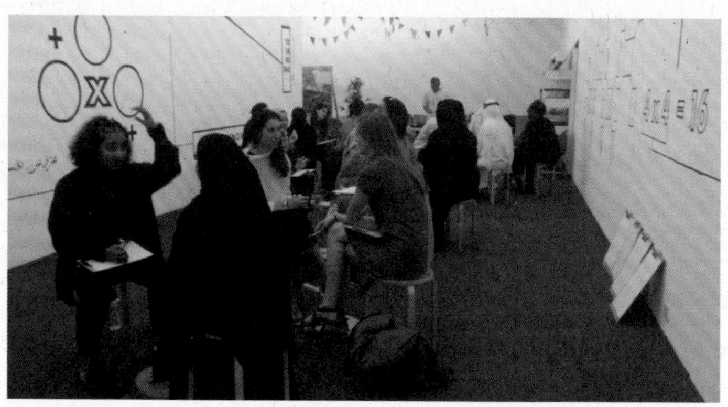

4

Fig. 1 : Outline of the *Speculative Collective* approach
Fig. 2–8: Participatory setting in the installation *Speculative Collective* during the Sharjah Biennial 14, 2019

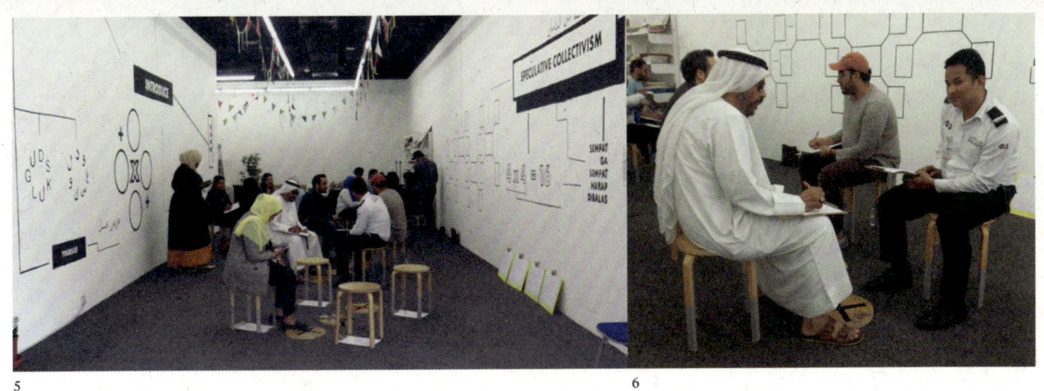

5

6

CERTIFICATE
SPECULATIVE COLLECTIVE X SHARJAH BIENNIAL 14 (2019)
شهادة
عمل جماعي تأملي * بينالي الشارقة 14 2019

is given to:
تمنح إلى
Post · Country Chicks

For the contribution and participation in proposing ideas for their speculative project:
لمساهمته/ لمساهمتها في طرح الأفكار ضمن مشروعهم التأملي
The "where are you from" answer of questions tool kit

May the spirit of Speculative Collective sustain.
لتعميم روح العمل الجماعي التأملي

2019

GUDSKUL
غودسكول
(MC Pringgotm)

Sharjah Art Foundation
مؤسسة الشارقة للفنون
SHARJAH ART FOUNDATION
( )

7

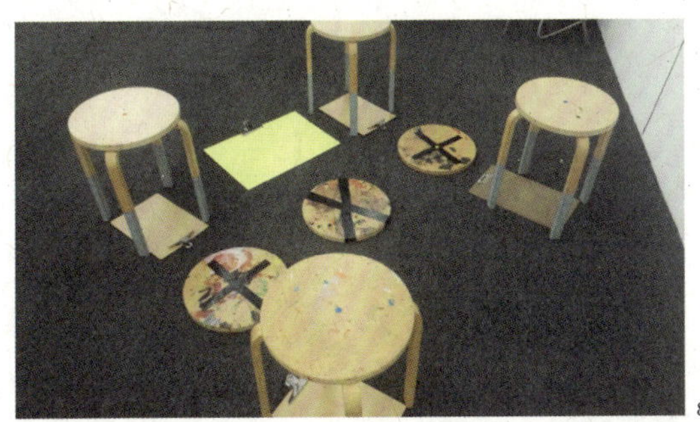

8

TOGETHER

IT TASTES BETTER.

RUANGRUPA

ruangrupa is a Jakarta-based collective founded in 2000. It is a non-profit organization committed to promoting art in urban contexts by engaging external artists as well as other disciplines such as social sciences, politics, technology, and media. They create their work with a view to nurturing critical perspectives on contemporary urban issues. ruangrupa collectively develops festivals, concerts, exhibitions, biennials, art labs, workshops, research, books, journals, magazines and online journals. Since 2020 they have been working on the artistic direction of the documenta fifteen in 2022.

THE COLLECTIVE EYE

The Collective Eye (TCE), founded 2012 in Montevideo, organizes exhibitions and symposia on collective practice in art. The collective has pursued a partnership with DISTANZ since 2021, publishing the book series *Thoughts on Collective Practice* as an extended collective between the publishing team and TCE. The first three volumes in the series discuss practices of collective action with the artist duo Elmgreen & Dragset, the collective Slavs and Tatars, originally founded as a reading group, and the theater director Roberto Ciulli. The volume of conversations with ruangrupa is the fourth installation in the series. TCE works to strengthen polynational dialogues between different collectives as well as between collectives and theorists.

THE COLLECTIVE EYE
Thoughts on Collective Practice
In Conversation with ruangrupa

PUBLISHED BY
DISTANZ Verlag
www.distanz.com

ISBN 978-3-95476-466-2

Printed in Germany

EDITORS
The Collective Eye / Dominique Lucien Garaudel, Heinz-Norbert Jocks, Emma Nilsson; and Matthias Kliefoth

CONCEPT
The Collective Eye, thecollectiveeye.org
and DISTANZ Verlag

DESIGN
Running Water Creative Group
runnigwater.eu

MAIN CONVERSATION
The Collective Eye / Heinz-Norbert Jocks, Dominique Lucien Garaudel
Text: Heinz-Norbert Jocks

PROJECT CONVERSATIONS AND TEXTS
THE KUDA
Singapore Night Festival
Matthias Kliefoth
SONSBEEK '16: transACTION
Emma Nilsson
Speculative Collective, Sharjah Biennale
Ok. Video – Jakarta International Video Art Festival
Victoria Tarak

COPY EDITING
Matthias Kliefoth, Charlotte Riggert / DISTANZ Verlag

TRANSLATION
Stanton Taylor / Good & Cheap Art Translators

TRANSCRIPTION
Alexandra Skwara

PHOTO CREDITS
Portrait, p. 2: Jin Panji
Gudskul, pp. 60-63, 98-99, 150-153:
ruangrupa & Gudskul archives
All other images: ruangrupa archives

PRODUCTION MANAGEMENT
Charlotte Riggert, Rebecca Wilton / DISTANZ Verlag

PRINTING AND BINDING
optimal media GmbH, Röbel/Müritz

DISTRIBUTION
Edel Germany GmbH
International-books@edel.com